"I love her work, wisdom, and humor."
Anne Lamott, author, *Bird by Bird*

"If you've never read Mary Hayes Grieco before, you're in for such a treat I almost envy you. This is delicious wisdom and the finest quality writing. Mary is optimistic and passionate about the struggles, silliness, and successes we all experience on the path of everyday enlightenment."
Rosanne Bane, author, *Dancing in the Dragon's Den*

"I *love* Mary's inspirational book! It's perfect. Beautiful. Elegant. Useful. It is a wonderful holiday gift."
Andrew Ramer, author, *Ask Your Angels*

"These little essays share laughter, wonder, self-examination, growth, and loss—everything that goes into the sensational stew called living. Love it!
Minneapolis Star and Tribune

"Mary's style is a cross between Erma Bombeck and Joseph Campbell—it's where the kitchen sink and the cosmos come together."
Bobbie, a fan

To all my teachers, with all my love,

I offer this book.

BE A LIGHT

Illumined Essays for Times Like These

by

Mary Hayes Grieco

Waterwheel Publishing
Minneapolis, Minnesota

Published and distributed by:
Waterwheel Publishing
Post Office Box 7062
Minneapolis, Minnesota 55407-0062
www.waterwheelpublishing.com
admin@waterwheelpublishing.com

Book Design by Fred Grieco
Cover Design and Layout by Rene Erickson
Photo of the Author by Ann Marsden
With thanks to Carl George for his generous support

Publisher's Cataloging-in-Publication
(Provided by Quality Books, Inc.)
        Hayes-Grieco, Mary.
          Be a light : illumined essays for times like these /
        by Mary Hayes Grieco.
          p. cm.
          LCCN 2008930030
          ISBN-13: 978-0-9818200-8-8
          ISBN-10: 0-9818200-8-5
          ISBN-13: 978-0-9818200-9-5
          ISBN-10: 0-9818200-9-3

          1. Spiritual life.   I. Title.

BL624.H374 2008   204'.4
                              QBI08-600168

Essays

INTRODUCTION

"There are no strangers—only friends we haven't met yet." - Irish proverb

Hello, friend. I hope you will enjoy these essays, and that they will serve you well for a long time. I wrote these pieces at different times over the last twenty years, not because I had an idea that I was a writer or that this would ever be a book, but because at the time I wrote each one, I was trying to bring myself out of some kind of darkness into clarity and peace of mind, and writing helped me to do that. It was a pleasant surprise to me and a happy by-product of this activity that my writing turned out to be helpful to others as well. In 1992 my essays were discovered and published as a collection by Hazelden in a darling daily inspiration book, *The Kitchen Mystic: Spiritual Lessons Hidden in Everyday Life*. This book, *Be A Light*, is a reincarnation of that book—revised, updated, and expanded with ten new pieces. In a way, the first book was accidental, and this one is intentional.

I imagine that you, like me, wish to shed your fears and limitations, groom your best self into being, and shine like the sun—illumined by your soul and its loving purposes. So many of us around the world these days are waking up and committing ourselves to the goal of spiritual enlightenment. But human life is difficult—riddled with obstacles, losses, and unexpected trauma. And even if we have the good fortune to enjoy a gracious external life, we can still be painfully engaged with an internal struggle as we attempt to address our shortcomings or excesses of character. My personal struggles have been both external and internal: I've had to cope with a certain amount of loss and trauma throughout my life, and I've had to master my temperament, an extra-sensitive and high-maintenance personality that gets mired in insecurity and derailed by intense emotions and leftover ghosts from the past. I've done my best to make good use of my sensitivity, and gain what wisdom I can from my pain, and I have found a measure of peace with these facts of my existence.

I believe in human greatness. I have looked

it in the eyes a few times, in the presence of my spiritual teachers. I found their state of consciousness and their world service so inspiring that I became determined to attain my own greatness, whatever that looks like. I can't settle for less than that. Since I was young, I hungered for a meaningful purpose. Over time I discovered that my life purpose is to learn and to teach the ways of UNCONDITIONAL LOVE AND FORGIVENESS. Teaching forgiveness became my workaday job when I started teaching forgiveness workshops and classes in 1990, and it still is today. All the pain and struggle of my earlier life becomes meaningful when I view it as an excellent training program for my career as a healer and philosopher. More importantly, in UNCONDITIONAL LOVE AND FORGIVENESS I discovered the spiritual practices that give me my own best shot at ultimate freedom. I think I can get there from here, if I remain dedicated to it. I know that your life is imbued with your soul's purposes, and I believe that you too will discover how to end your suffering, find meaning, and become free.

The notion of human greatness was first

kindled for me when I was a girl reading *The Lives of the Saints* in the sheltered shadows of the staircase in my family's home. It was a home that was filled with both tender love and terrible alcoholic chaos. When I grew up, that little flame of vision was fanned into a blaze as I stood in awe at a fire ceremony conducted by Brahman priests at the home of my meditation teacher in India. That ceremony was dedicated to a Goddess whose mission is to end the ills of society. Later, my burning passion for illumination and world service was recognized, contained, and guided by my mentor, Dr. Edith Stauffer. With loving dispassion, she showed me exactly how to heal my wounds. She charged me to carry her life work, UNCONDITIONAL LOVE AND FORGIVENESS, into the world, and it became my work. This fire became steady and sealed into my cells with the firm touch of her aged hand upon my hand. This fire glows in the morning in the votive candle on the altar next to my chair when I meditate. It simmers on the stove as I make dinner for my family. It secretly informs my forgiveness workshops. The workshops are crafted out of a succession of seemingly ordinary moments and activities that build a field of light and love until something breaks open and an extraordinary experience is there for everyone in the room. It heals their pain. Now, this fire wants to be a book again.

The journey to liberation is by nature a challenging one—a hero's journey—and it requires the presence of dedicated traveling companions and frequent doses of inspiration and encouragement. Throughout the years, my path has been lit by the daily presence of an inspiring book—a book that is a friend that reflects myself back to me like a mirror, and keeps me company. I have always treasured a book written by someone who engaged life fully, and who was able to distill their personal experience into words that are universal and that shine with the golden nobility of something we call *truth*. When I was in high school, I was a lonely philosopher and an oddball who was warmly befriended by Henry David Thoreau and Kahlil Gibran. I traipsed through the crowded halls with a battered copy of *Walden Pond* or *The Prophet* in my purse, and

I pulled over to a private space at least once a day to find solace in reading and to find myself again. When I traveled around America in my early twenties, it was Walt Whitman's *Song of Myself* that lived in my backpack and spoke with me at bedtime, wherever that turned out to be. When I was in my thirties and forties, I found comfort and guidance in the *Bhagavad-Gita*, and reveled in several different translations. Now I'm in my fifties, and as I sit in my favorite chair and write this, there is a copy of *The Power of Now* nearby that is starting to show signs of much use.

Over these last 20 years I have been blessed to meet many people who loved my first book, *The Kitchen Mystic*, and who hoped to buy more copies of it. (It seems like no one who stumbled across it ever bought fewer than four copies of it.) These friendly fans like to show me their copy of my little book: dog-eared, streaked with yellow highlighter, and with their own enthusiastic notes scribbled in the margins. These strangers touch my arm with surprising intimacy, and look at me knowingly as they quote me to myself, as if we are old friends, meeting again. They lean into my face and tell me earnestly how loyal they feel to my little book, and how faithfully it's been there for them: *I keep it by my bedside .... I always take it with me on vacation .... It's on the kitchen counter where I can see it .... Here it is, right here in my purse, like it always is!* With a thrill of understanding, I see that my book is their *friend*, a trusted companion along the bumpy road to spiritual enlightenment. I feel so honored. When I look at those worn and tattered copies of *The Kitchen Mystic*, I am reminded of my own relationship with those few special books in my life, and I have come to think of my accidental first book as a "keeper," or as they call it in the publishing world, a "perennial." With so many old friends out there already, I mused, perhaps it is time for a reincarnation.

So, friend. I pray that *Be A Light: Illumined Essays for Times Like These* will be a good companion to you along your daily way, and that together we will walk with the inspiring company of great people who have gone before us. The well-loved masters, mystics, and social heroes of the past have held their illumined hearts out to

the world around them like a lamp in the darkness, and so can we. Thank God we are not alone,
you and I. We are together, your heart and mine,
with everyone else in the Great Heart that beats
in the center of Creation for all of us.

Mary Hayes Grieco
Autumn, 2008

A Creation Story

In the beginning, there was nothing. It was The Void, the only inhabitant of cold eternity. Then there was a spark! An impulse for something. It sprang into being, and tumbled and ricocheted around, multiplying itself a thousandfold in an instant. The sparks became a sound, a vast breathing sound, inhaling and exhaling in the darkness. The sound became Light, an infinite field of light. Without birth, without death, it always was.

The Light awakened to its own Self. It was the Great Self, a vast field of light illuminated from within by love. The primordial sound sang endlessly in its heart. *I wish to create!* Spirit said, and it breathed out a Universe in an instant with a *Bang!* Galaxies and worlds spun into being in a great dance. There were worlds and worlds— some cold, some molten, some with delicate little veils of atmosphere. One of the worlds was Gaia, blue-green and virginal. *You are special to me*, Spirit thought. *I will mate with you. I will impregnate you with my essence. You will bear me a child, in a form that reflects my own nature.*

Gaia conceived. The single cell in the womb of her oceans multiplied and grew, like a tadpole, like a frog, like a dinosaur, like a bird, like a mammal. It roared like a lion, climbed like an ape, and sang like a whale. It diversified and improvised, and the web of life was woven with intricacy, with texture and color, with lively and impeccable balance.

When the moment was right, the human beings emerged. In the heart of the human beings was the sound of God. In their breath was the tiny essence of the Great Spirit, the great breath. In the brain of the humans was a dormant center of light, awaiting the moment of kindling. In their nervous systems was the complex communications network between Spirit and form, the pathway of light into matter. In the DNA of the human being is the plan for God to wake up and know Himself, to express Herself, to live a loving, dynamic life in material form. Inside my own self God is waking up, stretching painfully through the slow rocky density of matter ... clumsily transcending the emotional heritage of my ancient defensive systems to remember the peace of my essence.

There is a divine spark of that great Light embodied as a soul in the small self of every human being. We see the light of the soul expressed as a certain spiritual quality in the personality: love, kindness, generosity, will, joy, patience. The Great Spirit looks sleepily out of my eyes, out of your eyes, in ever-increasing numbers of people around the world—reaching within and then spreading outward to share the awareness that God dwells within me, as me, God dwells within you, as you. We are the children of God in the lap of the Earth. We are the Light. Let us create!

"And God saw that it was good."
- Book of Genesis

The Kitchen Mystic

I'd like to suggest a new name for the spirituality that has taken root and spread in modern society like a successful new plant species brought from the Old World to the New. I see it in myself and in seekers around me who have passed through and incorporated the gifts of different paths since the early 1970s. I see it in the plethora of books about spirituality in everyday life that hit the shelves throughout the 1990s—chicken soup for all kinds of souls. It is there in the eyes of spiritual people, inside church communities and outside them, who choose to practice religion on the terms of their own inner authority— taking and leaving certain elements of church doctrine without the fear that was present for us in the past. You could characterize it as a synthesis of common sense and the perennial wisdom from religions both East and West. But it's more than that.

There is a massive spiritual awakening occurring in humanity as we enter the new millennium, and it holds within it the possibility that we will create Eden on Earth in coming centuries, even though we presently struggle with terror that we may destroy ourselves instead. This spiritualization of humanity will eventually have a profound impact on all parts of our human existence, and this unsung revolution that we are in the middle of is so intuitive and decentralized that it cannot be named or stopped. The building blocks of a new world slip quietly into place every time a human being makes a conscious choice toward higher consciousness in the everyday dramas that occur at home and at work. Peace on Earth comes closer with every breath I take as I cook a meal with an intention to foster wholeness for those who eat my food.

This revolution in consciousness is too big to be named for what it really is on the macro level, so I will give it a name for how it exists on the micro level, where each of us lives, day to day. I'll give it a homely name, for the kind of enlightenment most of us will attain is pretty homely. I'll call it Kitchen Mysticism. This garden-variety spiritual illumination is spreading all around us, and it is attained by each of us when we choose to be loving, present, and connected to all that is here in this very moment on this ordinary day. It is the life of the householder saint, the life of the Kitchen Mystic.

Formerly we have thought of mystics as rare people living in ecstatic solitude in a cave or forest, but really anyone is capable of mysticism if you look at an old concept freshly. The dictionary defines mysticism as "the belief in the direct, intimate union of the soul with God, through contemplation and love." The kitchen is where you perform important mundane acts such as cooking, eating, washing dishes, and telling the truth with your close friends. Kitchen Mysticism is a path that cultivates the awareness of direct, intimate union with the Divine in the arena of everyday mundane existence. It's a personal spiritual path, and there are as many ways of walking it as there are individuals.

The Kitchen Mystic may or may not attend an organized church because she finds so many everyday places to commune and worship: the shower, the car, the park bench at sunset. You will often spot the Mystic muttering earnestly aloud to Someone no one else can see, or stopping mid-project with an entranced look on their faces ... listening .... They are performing one of the major practices of the Faith: conducting an ongoing loving dialogue between the God Within and the God Without.

Kitchen Mystics have rich internal life, and so we have a smaller appetite for external stimulation than people who are not yet mystics. We pay for entertainment less and less because we see that truth is stranger than fiction anyway. A passionate spiritual seeker finds himself involved in a never-ending mystery story that is unfolding with subtlety, finesse, and occasional high drama. There is a benevolent plot afoot and the conspirators are everywhere, seen and unseen. Their mission: the total destruction of my fear and limitation, and my final spiritual awakening! It's harrowing, it's uplifting, and more thrilling than any action movie because I myself am the main character! We Kitchen Mystics keep each other vastly entertained with accounts of the latest synchronicity and breakthrough insights we are experiencing.

Mystics find meaning in many places. God is always hiding clues and love letters for us in the people and scenery of daily life, and it's fun to discover these—kind of like an Easter egg hunt. I wink and nod at my Friend when I have found another colored egg, and we laugh together at the humor and cleverness with which it was hidden in plain sight. If I am struggling to uncover a new understanding, I feel It whispering to me: "You're getting warm ... warmer ... cooler ... warmer ... HOT!" I will eventually get it or be taken gently by the hand and helped before I get dejected.

Almost every Kitchen Mystic has a special object of contemplation and worship, something from the physical world that says, "God" directly to you—and maybe nobody else! Over the years I have heard that the gate to the perfection of the Universe is flung open for the mystic by the sight of a seashell, a flower, a pine cone, a starry night, a flowing stream, or the fathomless gaze of an infant. What's your favorite holy object?

One of my daughters sees the Divine in a common rock. When she was tiny and I was trying to hustle her into the car to go to daycare, she would stop several times as we crossed the street to pick up stones and talk to them, and put them in her pockets. When we returned from traveling, her suitcase rattled with the inevitable stones that called out to her as new friends. She won't let me dispose of them—they're sacred. White ones are extra special, and she can spot a chip of white quartz in a bag of common fish tank gravel and insist that I meditate on it with her. "Mom, look at that white one," she says in a hushed, reverent voice. "Um ... wow!" I say, feigning understanding. Personally, I don't *get* God in rocks, but I feel it is important for mystics to support each other's contemplation.

I see God in onions. I always have. I remember when I first saw my mother slicing into an onion when I was about six. I stopped my playing, awestruck. What *is* this vegetable that is so pure, so watery-white, so many-layered in concentric rings that makes mounds of perfect circles that fall open onto the cutting board? I begged her to let me cut some, despite her warning that it would make my eyes burn. I can remember the concentration and reverence welling up within me as I awkwardly tried to make perfect slices. My eyes *did* burn and I had to stop after a few cuts, but I vowed that I would understand onions some day, and cook with them myself.

Later that summer my Dad took us all out for a rare visit to a fast-food joint—a real treat. My younger brothers and sisters ordered hamburgers with ketchup, but my Dad turned to me and said, "How about it, honey—you want everything on it?"

"Everything on it ...." Those words struck me like a sacred gong, a mantra given to me personally that would guide me all of my days. I nodded mutely, not even understanding what these words meant in your usual hamburger joint—I only knew that this *was* a spiritual risk I was destined to take. When my hamburger arrived, I peeked under the soggy bun and was thrilled to see the chopped grilled onions sprinkled like tiny translucent pearls amid the steaming ketchup, mustard, and pickles. I ate my burger in a blissful trance, convinced that I would eat them with "everything on it" forevermore.

My contemplation of the Mystery in the onion continues to this day. As an artist, I paid homage to my friend the onion by creating a stained glass window of an underground bulb that now hangs in a local store. As a cook, I have learned how to coax the sweetness out of an onion, and to tame its fire into mellow good humor. I can cut them now without crying, but not without pausing for a brief moment of worship. Red onions are especially divine. I hold a slice up to the sunlight pouring in through the kitchen window, and it glows like a fine piece of antique glass. Cool watery white with layers delicately edged with imperial purple ... strong, humble, peaceful ... with that fiery nub of spring green in the center aspiring to sprout and become more .... "Ah! Look at *this* one!" I cry to my husband and daughter. They look at each other and smile at me with loving tolerance. "That's a really nice one, Mom," my daughter replies in a soothing tone of voice, and my husband nods vigorously, demonstrating support. They don't *get* God in onions the way I do, but they know that we mystics have to stick together.

"Sultan, saint, pickpocket—love has everyone by the ear, drawing us to God by secret ways. I never knew that God, too, desires us."

- Rumi

SPIRITUALITY AND RELIGION

"Don't throw the baby out with the bath water," the old saying goes. This is a valuable saying when it comes to spirituality and religion. In recent years I have heard some former churchgoers say, "I'm a recovering Catholic," as if referring to a dangerous disease. And I know that some traditional churches give their congregations dire warnings about any kind of spiritual exploration that is not strictly based in the Christian Bible. They view other paths as scattered and shallow, or worse, the direct conspiracy of the devil! I believe that it is unnecessary to have such a polarization between traditional religion and a personal, open-ended spiritual search. There is a need today for both of these things, and I think it's time for us to be clear about the distinctiveness and the value of both spirituality and religion.

What *is* the distinction between spirituality and religion? There certainly is one. All of us have known detestable people who went to church every Sunday, as well as kind, gentle souls who never entered a church in their lives. Religion, in and of itself, doesn't produce spiritual people. And spiritual people grow and unfold something beautiful whether they're in a church or not.

Spirituality is the cultivated awareness that I am an individual expression of an immortal Being whose nature is love, peace, and creativity. Let's take this apart to understand it fully. *Awareness* is defined as "being cognizant, conscious, knowing, especially in a keenly responsive way." It is a state of being and perception rather than a collection of beliefs. *A cultivated awareness* is a state of awareness that you deliberately grow, like a gardener. You develop it with education and training, helpful techniques and ongoing attention.

"An individual expression of an immortal Being" means that I am a small but important part of something much greater than I. There is something that was here before I became who I am now, and it will exist after I lay this body and personality down at my death. I am that something, that Self, temporarily expressing itself here in this time. This Self is also expressing itself all

around me as the different people, creatures, and objects that make up what we call the world. Like water in the ocean, we are defined as drops for a short time, but we are always a part of the ocean that exists before, during, and after a drop or wave expresses itself individually. The nature of the Self is love, peace, and creativity. It has many other qualities too. These are the spiritual qualities that religions have attempted to instill for ages: faith, hope, joy, compassion, courage, kindness, universal brotherhood, and strength.

The challenge of our spiritual journey is to heal and clarify the personality on all levels (physical, emotional, mental, and spiritual) so that we can experience these spiritual qualities, not just hope for and think about them. We think we are human beings seeking a divine experience, but the key to our liberation is the realization that we are divine Beings having a human experience. We are Spirit, enjoying a risky sojourn as a higher mammal here on planet Earth.

Our bodies and psyches are thick and dark with pain and ignorance, like a lamp with a blackened glass chimney. As St. Paul wrote:

"We see as through a glass, darkly." The spiritual journey is the cleaning and polishing of the glass so that the burning light within may radiate outward, illuminating itself and its environment. As we become enlightened we embody more and more energy and happiness in our direct knowledge that we are an expression of God. Anything we do in our daily lives to cultivate more of this love, peace, and creativity is a spiritual practice. Spirituality is a personal matter, and every one of us has a completely unique spiritual journey.

Spirituality is a state of relaxed loving presence to the Self, to others, to Nature, and to Spirit. It is the experience of being fully present and alive within a circle of Life—safe and whole and completely provided for in a spacious sense of the *Now*. After all, the beginning and the end of the spiritual journey is the present moment: there is nowhere to go but Here, and there's nobody here but one Self, which holds everyone in the Universe inside a web of interconnection.

A religion is a prescribed path for spiritual exploration. It is a container for spiritual experience that arises out of—and contributes to—a cultural context. Religion provides a seeker with community, ritual, rules, limits, mythology, inspired writings, spiritual practices, and models of spiritual mastery. Every true religion has a living wellspring of transforming spiritual energy at its center, sometimes originating from the life and spirit of a great master (Jesus, Buddha, etc.) who was a light in his own time and still is in ours. A living religion is whole within itself, and is internally consistent. There is an overall balance and integrity to the path which brings depth and richness to a seeker as they mature.

When you "subscribe" to a religion, you enter a circle of spiritual experience, and the archetypes and the personality of the religion will influence the kind of growth experiences you will have. If you become a Buddhist, you will have "Buddhist-flavored" experiences. You will engage with the notion that everything is impermanent, and you will be challenged to increase your capacity for compassion. If you commit to the Christian religion, you will have a relationship with the Master Jesus, and learn about forgiveness and surrender.

When I took up a particular yoga practice, my life became influenced by Hindu archetypes, and I had some vivid dreams in which elephants figured prominently. I also had experiences in meditation in which I conversed with the teacher of the yoga tradition and received helpful guidance. My dreams and meditations were interesting to my fellow seekers in the yoga community, but I couldn't share them with my Catholic Mom and receive understanding and enthusiastic support. I felt lucky to have an interested community where I could share my inner journey.

The trouble with religion is that it is a human institution attempting to deliver the Divine to its constituents. It carries with it all the rigidities and complications that a collection of human egos can create together over time. Religions are subject to politics, distortion, and decay. This can become so severe that the original energy and inspiration that brought it into being is all but choked off. Hence the existence of churches that seem lifeless. There's nothing worse than attending a service at a dead church.

A dead church is one with an absence of genuinely inspired leadership, and a sad lack in the number of seekers that are enthusiastically practicing self-mastery. I think a lot of people go to church because it is part of their family's status quo. They are "hanging out" around the well and socializing, but are not willing to haul steadily on the ropes to bring up the water and drink. It is the *spiritual* people in a congregation that are working hard to make the religion real and meaningful, and the rest of the people watch them from a safe comfort zone. They will catch a sip or two of energy and insight as a by-product of the dedication of the spiritual athletes in their church. Maybe there's nothing wrong with that—it is the benefit of participating with a religious community.

Oftentimes the most enthusiastic participants in a church are the converts. They haven't had the religion forced on them since birth, and something of the fresh living Spirit reaches out and taps them on the shoulder. *"Come!"* it says, with a smile that speaks true in their heart. This is true for my cousin Betsy. She married a Muslim scholar and became a follower of Islam. She wholeheartedly embraced it, to the dismay of all her Catholic relatives and feminist friends. They shuddered with horror at her new practices— keeping her head veiled, disappearing for prayers three times a day, accepting her defined role as wife and mother. Betsy's social circle dwindled to practically nothing until it eventually began to expand into the Muslim community where her lifestyle was understood and accepted. I appreciate committed people of any flavor, so I was intrigued and went to visit her.

Betsy and I spent a good part of the day together in her small sunny apartment with our children. We talked about religion and our spiritual experiences. We wiped noses, and made peanut butter snacks (apparently a universal concept) for the kids. At precisely noon and precisely three o'clock, she disappeared for a few minutes of devotional prayer in the direction of Mecca. She moved in her small world with quiet grace and serene eyes, and demonstrated endless patience with her sticky, boisterous toddlers. She was happy. It was one of the most peaceful afternoons I had spent in a while, and as I took my leave, my heart was full and rosy. I was spiritually fed all day by a palpable glow of love and light that was established in their home because of their spiritual practices. That day, I enjoyed the mundane spirituality of motherhood in a new way, influenced by Betsy's total surrender to her path as a mother.

A lot of people these days are turning to Earth-based religions for a new dimension in their religious expression. Ordinary people who grew up Lutheran are attending Native American pipe ceremonies, dancing a spiral dance at a Wiccan solstice, or seeking power animals to the beat of drums in a shamanic journey. There is an important recognition going on: it is necessary to come once again into sacred relationship with our Mother Earth. There is a turning towards religions where God is seen and celebrated as *immanent*, here inside of us and in the land—not *transcendent* in a far-away place called Heaven.

This awareness is necessary for balance, but indigenous leaders caution us. They don't want us to casually strip-mine their religions without real awareness and respect for it. Don't do a sweat because it's "cool" and your friends are doing it. Do a sweat because your own inner Spirit says, "You are ready for this. Bare your heart ... prepare to give and receive ... enter the Mystery and offer up your fears." Native elders often say to Christians, "Turn to your own roots. There is power there. There is Spirit. Go to the roots of your own religion and make it belong to you."

I took their advice and looked to my own Catholic tradition. I've always maintained a heartfelt connection with Jesus and Mary despite the fact that I couldn't stand to go to church for many years. It made me feel tight in my chest and stomach, so I trusted my body's wisdom and stayed away. But I privately took Jesus, Mary, and the Holy Spirit along with me. My spiritual life found expression in a yoga meditation practice, and solstice and equinox rituals in women's circles. One day I stumbled upon a Catholic church that was rocking with spirit, community, and an independent consciousness that promotes women's leadership in the church, among other worthy notions. I went back to church and settled into a synthesis of my religious roots and my modern explorations: and so a committed Catholic-Yogic-Goddess worshiper I remain. It is my own form of Trinity, a braid of religious practice and understanding. I feel good about this. It's big enough for breathing room yet small enough for focus and consistency. Each strand of my braid contributes to the power and effectiveness of the others. And they all lead me deeper into wholeness—into relaxed, loving presence to myself, to others, to Nature, and to God, as I choose to understand Her.

I am not alone in my self-made religion. Recently I went on a lovely retreat to a small Franciscan center run by two nuns. As I sat in their cozy living room by the fire, my eyes and my heart found rest in the pictures of Jesus and Mary that hung on the walls. The sun shone like fiery jewels through a round stained glass window that depicted a female form holding up the moon. As one of the sisters moved quietly through the room, I caught the wholesome scent of almond fragrance in sesame oil—she had just given someone a therapeutic massage. While I did not hear the click of swinging rosary beads as I used to in school, I was still reminded of those nuns of my childhood. I thought of them with love, as women with ideals, women with personal discipline, women living in community. Religious beliefs aside, they were then the kind of women I like to be with today. I remembered how hard they worked to instill the strength of religion in my soul. I realized with amazement that they had succeeded. I saw this modern sister go to the bookcase and pick up her Motherpeace Tarot cards. She was going to her room to meditate near her statue of St. Francis. I watched the fire in the silent sunlit room, and realized I was home.

I believe deeply that we must find, all of us together,
a new spirituality.
This new concept ought to be elaborated
alongside the religions,
in such a way that all people of good will
could adhere to it.
We need a new concept, a lay spirituality.
We ought to promote this concept,
with the help of scientists.
It could lead us to set up what we are all looking for:
a secular morality.
I believe in it deeply.
And I think we need it so the world
can have a better future.
- The 14ᵗʰ Dalai Lama

WOMEN'S SPIRITUALITY

In ancient times, God was perceived and worshiped as female, The Divine Mother. Women were valued as leaders and contributors in society because of our close connection to the Creator through our intuition, through our connection with Nature, and through our creative and procreative abilities. Women today are leading a movement in modern society that will benefit men and women alike: the rebirth of respect for the feminine principle within ourselves and in all of our institutions.

I was raised in the Catholic church, and when I was a girl I wanted to grow up to be a priest. I remember playing "Mass" with my brothers and my friends, and always vying for that special role. I wanted to be the one who respectfully held the holy chalice aloft, and shared wise words at the sermon, the one who held her hands out in blessing at the end of the service. But I was told that I could never do that because girls were not allowed to be priests. Why? It baffled me. The boys I knew weren't even interested in the job. It was something about how Eve made a mistake a long time ago ... or was it because Jesus' apostles were all male? What was it? I couldn't get a satisfying answer to any of my questions, no matter how hard I tried.

I have been a seeker of truth all my life, even as a child, and I actually did pay attention in church. I listened to the priest's sermons, and tried to apply the truth of what he was saying to my own life. I remember being in church one morning and standing in the back near a pillar, listening to the priest speaking. I can't recall his exact words that day, but I'll never forget how deeply they wounded me. He said something casually, almost like a joke or an afterthought, about the inferiority of females. The offhanded words of my parish priest insinuated that we women are intrinsically weaker and spiritually less developed than men because of our gender. He said those terrible lies from the pulpit, as a spiritual authority, and no one in the congregation challenged him. I wish that someone there had leaped to their feet and called out, "Ex*cuse* me, Father! That last statement of yours was pretty sexist!" But it was 1966, and no one yet possessed the concept or the vocabulary to say that to him. Therefore his words struck my heart and my belly like a knife, plunging a feeling of shame and rage down into my soul in an instant. Something shut down in me at that moment. I simultaneously closed myself off from the Church and from God and from my own female nature for many years. I count that moment as a wound to my essential self, one of the times in my development when I lost a chunk of power that I spent some effort to retrieve when I was an adult and in the business of restoring myself to wholeness.

But today I count myself as fortunate because I live in a time when I can heal the wounds of oppression that are specific to women. Okay, so I had to do a bit of therapy about it, but at least no one's hauling me off to be burned at the stake any time soon. And thanks to the most recent wave of the women's movement, women as a group have challenged the basic assumptions of what we call patriarchy, the male-dominated mind-set that has shaped societies around the world for several thousand years. There has been a lot written in the last thirty-five years that helps us to understand what the premises and the ways of the patriarchal mind-set are, with all the good and all the harm that has been created through its power structures. Through the skillful scholarship of women theologians, historians, and archeologists, we are coming to a point where we can see that humanity has traveled a full circle. The Divine Mother is returning to us.

A new mind-set, influenced by Her rising energy, is emerging—a body of informed values that is at once ancient and revolutionary. It has been incubating in circles of women since the early 1970s, and showing up shyly at workshops and conferences throughout the 1980s and 1990s. It is rolling off the bookshelves into the mass psyche through fictional best-sellers like *The Mists of Avalon, The Red Tent,* and *The Da Vinci Code.* The modern stories of the ancient respect for the Divine Feminine offer us a memory that is also a vision: a world in which feminine strength is respected and in which we develop peaceful and ecologically sustainable societies in the unfolding millennium. This set of values has grown in definition and confidence, and now it stands calmly at the doors of all of our institutions—churches, government, schools, and the workplace—awaiting the time for a radical shift in how things are done. Some people call this point of view "women's spirituality." Those of us who have followed an eclectic spiritual path for a while have a sense of what we mean by this, but let's get more real about it. What exactly is women's spirituality?

Women's spirituality is the cultivated awareness of God as Divine Mother, immanent in ourselves and in the Earth around us. It is a respectful consciousness of the interconnectedness of all life, and the sacred honoring of all phases of created life, from birth to death. If we look through the lens of "women's spirituality" and assume it actually is an integrated body of spiritual values and practices, we see that it is comprised of the following characteristics:

Women's spirituality is an expression of the ancient earth-based spirituality that was widespread in human culture the world over before the rise of the patriarchy. It is still present in Native American culture and all forms of shamanism that still exist in the villages of indigenous people everywhere. It is rising again today as Wicca, the reincarnation of the European earth-based religion.

Women's spirituality takes the point of view that God is immanent, or present, in the world and in our own beings. This is the opposite and complementary point of view of the traditional patriarchal religious viewpoint that God is transcendent, or beyond this world. This earth-based point of view is the balancing counterpoint to the transcendent forms of religion, which have grown too "heady"—too disconnected from the body and the Earth.

Women's spirituality cultivates the awareness that God is Female, the Divine Mother, or Goddess, as well as God the Father, and that God guides us directly through feelings and intuition, as well as through reason.

Women's spirituality assumes a Universe that is unified and benevolent, and that people too are essentially good. In this model, although evil exists as part of life, the duality of good and evil rests within a larger unity which is benevolent. In other words, the "war" between good and evil is only a small facet of what is going on in the Universe, not the main play. There is no ultimate devil battling God to own my individual soul, and there is no original sin that a human being needs to be released from by a church in order to be a worthy citizen of Life.

Women's spirituality is the consciousness of connection and interconnection. The goal of this way of life is to become established in a state of loving respect for all of life. I foster my connection with all of the communities that I ever become aware of: angels, people from other cultures, plants and animals—even insects. The Native Americans, with their universal sense of connectedness, referred to insects as "the little people of the air," and knew that we must peacefully coexist. This ecological consciousness was one that humans knew in ancient times and our species needs to embrace it again, wholeheartedly.

Within the paradigm of women's spirituality time is round and cyclical, as well as linear. Time moves through the cycles of the moon, the seasons, and our own body's clock. Women have always been connected to what Ann Wilson Schaef refers to as "round time." We are linked to the cycles of the moon, and the rhythms of our children's physical needs. When we have a baby, life becomes a lot about the times when they eat, sleep, and need their diapers changed. We experience a stressful clash when we are forced to leave round time and our babies for many hours at our linear-time jobs.

The Earth herself lives in round time, and her consciousness changes with her body's phases, responding to the pull of the moon on her tides, and her daily and seasonal alignment to the sun. People used to celebrate the Earth's changes in time by gathering for rituals at spring and fall equinox and winter and summer solstice. People today who are intuitively moving back into earth-based spirituality create modern gatherings to do the same thing.

Women's spirituality holds sexuality as sacred. Sexuality is a healthy expression of pleasure and worship, and an act of love and celebration! We are all in the business of retrieving the gifts of that intimate experience from the repression and shame that shadows our sexuality because of centuries of distorted teachings from a misguided patriarchal church. Sex is Nature's gift to us for procreation, of course, but Nature must have intended it to be so much more for human beings or She wouldn't have made it so complex and so much fun! There are so many ways we can engage in sex with another person, different than frogs and dogs, and one of those ways is to allow it to be the ecstatic dance of God and Goddess, renewing the world again and again.

In women's spirituality, a woman's fertility and all passages of her fertility cycle are sacred, and marked with honoring ceremonies. Menstruation, sexual initiation, birth, menopause, the advent of the wisdom of the old crone—all are important passages of a woman's spiritual journey in her body, and women today are reclaiming those rites of passage from our ancient memory of when the Goddess governed our lives. As more and more of us celebrate the onset of menstruation with our girls, and bring the midwife's gentle influence back into our hospital birth practices, we reinstate the glory and dignity of women's fertility. Now, Baby Boomer women call hot flashes "power surges" and encourage each other to fearlessly express our purposes long into old age.

Fertility is a spiritual force, and I'm glad that the sacredness of fertility is starting to be restored in our culture. Growing up in America, which is a workaholic and productivity-driven culture, I was taught to look at menstruation as a messy inconvenience, and something that makes women flawed and less reliable as leaders. But if we look at it with sacred eyes, we might see that menstruation gives women a wisdom advantage: our increased sensitivity to the inner self, to Nature, and the collective consciousness at those times is an opportunity for powerful meditation and steady masterful growth. A Native American neighbor of mine still goes into her "moon lodge" symbolically when she menstruates. She stops cooking and tending her family, and retreats to her own space with a book and a journal for the first two days of her period. Her family members just pick up the slack and support her privacy, and no one even questions it. Lovely! We'd be so sane if we lived in round time again, as well as linear time. I think we modern women should learn about this ancient respectful consciousness from whatever sources are available to us.

Women's spirituality promotes creativity. Creativity is an expression of the self, working with the Creator to bring new things forth. Knitting, handwork, gardening, decorating—all traditional realms that belong to women—are expressions of creativity and worthy spiritual practices if we declare them to be.

As I discussed in my previous essay, spirituality is a personal matter, and each person's spiritual truth is developed by a direct experience of God in a mystical moment, and through a personal history of mystical moments. Everything I have learned about life through the lens of my female spirituality has come to me directly in a mystical moment ... in an encounter with an assertive spider in the woods ... as I danced ecstatically in a spiral of women singing *She changes everything She touches and everything She touches changes* ... when I leaned my sweaty head on my partner's flannel shirt and felt our hearts beating together as our baby slid out of my body into a new world sparkling with Presence ... when I was struck speechless by the sight of a red maple tree strung with thousands of delicate spider webs shimmering in bright October sunlight .... My spiritual experiences as a woman connected to myself and all of life are strung on a necklace of joy, bead by bead, story by story. I hope that when I lay my body down like an old husk after years of fearless crone-hood, my spirit will rise and humbly offer this necklace at the feet of a laughing Goddess.

This lover of love sings: Mother! Mother! Mother!
Who can fathom your mystery, Your eternal play of
love with love? Please make this poor poet madly
wealthy with the infinite treasure of your love
- Ramprasad

We will never lose our way
to the well of Her memory
and the power of Her living flame will rise—
it will rise again ...
- a Celtic Goddess Chant

Your Spiritual Teacher

A basic and universal tenet of the sturdy spiritual seeker is: *My life is a classroom. I am learning an important lesson from this experience.* This point of view encourages us to take responsibility for our actions and attitudes with the strength and humility of a master-in-training, instead of a victim of circumstance. We are always learning, if we are open to it. Sometimes we long for a good teacher to come and show us the way, and sometimes we are lucky enough to have a wise guide for a while. But whether there is a living teacher in front of us or not, we are never alone with our lessons, because we have a teacher inside us. The spiritual teacher that is within me is my own soul, providing circumstances and daily life instructors to foster my own wisdom.

When I look behind me on my journey, I see an unbroken daisy chain of people and events that have brought me to where I stand. If I open my eyes to my circumstances today, I recognize the class I am currently enrolled in, and feel the gentle encouraging smile of The Teacher.

mount of joy or suffering I experience in life is in direct proportion to the grace with which I accept my role as a student. I need to recognize the course I am enrolled in if I can, and apply myself to the work at hand with zest and humility. And I need to give honor and thanks to my teachers. Who are my teachers? My teachers are exactly the people and situations that I am engaged with today.

Relationships are teachers. My twenty-five year marriage feels like a tough graduate course: "Trust, Vulnerability, and Mutual Respect 300." My daughters and granddaughters are team-teaching "Life is Fun 101." My best friend cheerfully nudges me past the limited gates of my own thinking, and my rude neighbors help me ground the heady principles of UNCONDITIONAL LOVE AND FORGIVENESS into real life words and actions.

You can learn a lot about yourself from people who elicit a strong response from you, positive or negative. You can bet that these people are mirrors for your own greatness or for your flaws. Study your heroes. What seedling quality in yourself is in full flower in that person? Our heroes magnetize us to them to call forth our own embryonic excellence. We have teachers who facilitate our learning in a graceful and harmonious way, and we have teachers who deliver our lessons through the friction of our personality differences. But are we really different from each other?

Everyone has someone in their environment who is irritating, someone you just love to hate. They are a teacher. There used to be a woman in my life who was very annoying, and she just wouldn't go away. I bumped into her *everywhere*. After several years, I realized that this woman loudly demonstrated the same insecurities in me that I quietly hid from myself and others. I practiced compassion and acceptance towards her as a step in greater love for myself. I don't ever see her any more—I guess I don't need to.

Even an outright enemy is valuable. People who attack us provide us with a golden opportunity to develop more confidence, self-esteem, and boundaries, *fast*. Sometimes we don't tackle these lessons unless we really need to. Thanks, Teach. Benjamin Franklin once said, "Have gratitude for the presence of your enemies: they point out your flaws for you." The practice of gratitude is a good one to use in the face of people who make you very uncomfortable. Gratitude is one of the fastest tracks to the peace and strength of the Higher Self. If we can say, "Thank you for this opportunity to become more my Self"—and try to mean it—we make quick progress in the classrooms taught by our adversaries.

Some people wear the title, "teacher." In this case, they may be a real spiritual teacher or they may be a helpful technician. A technician is someone who has a tool or technique that you can learn quickly and apply to your life to some benefit, but the actual person soon fades into the background of your life. There are a lot of them around these days, peddling self-help books and seminars.

A spiritual teacher—someone who has truly become what they teach—is more rare. They walk their talk. They *are* what they teach—it radiates out of their pores. You find yourself wanting to just be with them, to watch them, to hang around after class. There is something there that you need to imprint upon, as a baby goose does with the mother goose before it too can fly. You carry these teachers in your heart all the days of your life.

I feel this way about one of my spiritual teachers, Edith, whom I met in 1986 when she was 76 and I was 31. I had the great fortune to meet this fabulous mentor when she was at the zenith of her life's wisdom, and to be her student and friend for nearly twenty years. Edith wrote and taught UNCONDITIONAL LOVE AND FORGIVENESS, and in her presence I saw love and grace in action, as well as the health benefits of living in a forgiving way. It was so beautiful to watch her live and work that I felt the need to follow her about to her workshops like a lovesick puppy for the first few years of our relationship, and to go visit her in her home for a week at a time every few years. I absorbed her teachings by osmosis. Edith modeled for me the serenity and abundant energy of someone who had no more inner conflicts. From morning to night she served the good of the whole world effortlessly, like a clear spring of water continuously bubbling forth.

As we grew together side by side over twenty years, she cheered me on as I mastered her life work, and entrusted me with carrying it forward when it was time for her to stop teaching. In fact, she humbly claimed that I surpassed her in the creativity with which I taught our workshops, and that she was glad about that. I know that some of Edith's basic happiness was the gift of having a naturally positive personality, but I also think her luminous clarity as a teacher and a healer were the result of her diligence as a student to the teachers in her life. I will always carry her in my heart.

My teacher inspired me to diligence in the classrooms that I found myself assigned to, and the classrooms I learned the most in were the difficult situations apparently not of my choosing—situations in which I had little external control. My tendency is to fret and complain and stubbornly resist dealing with anything new or painful. But I learned to collect myself and ask an important question: *What spiritual principle is being called for here? Patience? Tolerance? Faith? Truth? Courage? Kindness? What character strength is my inner teacher trying to develop in me at this time?*

I learned that the sooner I get clear on the assignment and surrender to it with zest and willingness, the sooner I feel happy about the whole thing. Then something beautiful emerges within me.

On the other hand, I've found that some learning is such that it takes a long time to unfold, and it is necessary to thrash along with trial and error for a while. Sometimes you're simply in the dark without matches. You can drive yourself mad asking yourself, "What lesson is this? What am I *supposed* to be learning?" Don't worry—you're learning. You're just in process, and you'll know when you know, and not before. Just keep doing what is right in front of you with as much love and focus as you can muster, and you can't go too far wrong!

Sometimes we just need to be in place and allow ourselves to be slowly and steadily opened by the hundreds of tiny duties and challenges that our responsibilities place before us each day. In my mind I see this process like the opening of a peony in June. It sits there on its long stalk with the life-force swelling upward into a hard round bud. And then along come the ants! Hundreds of tiny ants stream up the stem and swarm all over the bud, gently pestering the flower to uncurl her petals and let them in to experience her nectar. For over a week the ants make their way slowly inside the petals, layer after layer. They just keep tromping around in there, helping the flower to open fully to the sunlight. They are serving the life force. One day you look and there is this absolutely gorgeous flower breathing fragrance and color into space with unabashed extravagance. If you cut this perfect specimen and put it in a crystal vase on your table, you will still encounter quite a few dedicated ants!

Like the ants in the peony, there are some lessons in my life that will probably come in installments until the day I die—trust, vulnerability, intimacy .... On the other hand, there are a few courses that I know I have actually completed—I felt the smile of my Teacher as she put a star on my chart. At these rare and precious times, there is a sense of wholeness and completion, and I think I understand the freedom in the Native American declaration, "It is a good day to die!"

Kabir says: Listen, friend!
My beloved Master lives inside.

MAKE FRIENDS WITH DISCIPLINE

Happiness is a matter of personal discipline. Happiness is a stance that I choose, and I must build it and reinforce it on a daily basis whether I am in the mood to do it or not. If I don't practice the disciplines that produce happiness, my consciousness soon becomes as sordid and fearful as a bad movie. Who needs that if given a choice?

Many people are allergic to the term *discipline,* perhaps because it is falsely associated with another word—*punishment.* This is understandable, since many of us were abused as children in the name of discipline. But in truth, the practice of personal discipline is an act of self-love. It is the way we turn our backs on a long bleak history of abandonment and come home to ourselves. Making friends with discipline is one of the best things we can do for ourselves.

Discipline is a set of attitudes and behaviors that I choose and practice with persistence to produce long-term health and happiness—whether or not I feel happy about doing it in the short term.

A recovering alcoholic employs discipline to get to an A.A. meeting even though she doesn't feel like it. A parent who was abused as a child halts his knee-jerk response to hit his rebellious child, even though he really feels like it. We may need to turn to self-discipline because our lives have become unmanageable in some way, but discipline will become our lifelong companion if we are serious about self-mastery.

Self-mastery will come to us as a result of becoming disciplined on all levels of the self—physical, emotional, mental, and spiritual. On the physical level, this is establishing good health habits, being financially responsible, keeping beauty and order in our environment, and walking in balance with the natural world. On the emotional level it is handling feelings appropriately. We need to know how and when to feel, share, and release emotions, as well as when to detach from excessive sensitivity and emotionality. On the mental level, it is our responsibility to uproot negative conditioned beliefs in our minds and cultivate a positive, self-chosen world view.

Ultimately, we are meant to be the masters of our minds and not the servants—to focus our thoughts or be silent at will. This is the goal of the discipline of meditation. As we make progress with disciplines on different levels, our personalities become clean and luminous for the inner Spirit to shine through. On the spiritual level, we can operate with more and more love and power for the well-being of everyone. This is a long-term project, but I can't think of a better way to live a life.

It is usually obvious what area of life is calling for self-discipline. We feel out of control, frustrated, and ashamed. Or maybe we are in denial of the problem but we are getting consistent feedback from others that our lack of self-control is problematic for *them*. We are asked to make a change that feels unnatural to us. In his classic book, *The Road Less Traveled,* M. Scott Peck describes discipline as an "unnatural" act. It is certainly a radical act of the spiritual will. But if we make a commitment to an upward trend in our life, we will choose new attitudes and behaviors.

At first it feels like pushing a boulder uphill. Progress is infinitesimal or erratic for a while, but this is deceptive—a lot of growth goes on underground. It is better to make some small real changes than to make a big, heroic, noisy effort for several days and then completely forget about our commitment and backslide. That adds to our hopelessness about our ability to change.

It works best to practice a new discipline without being attached to immediate results. We will make incremental progress and leave crisis behind. If we persist in the effort, we begin to stabilize, and gain glimpses of health and mastery in this part of our lives. It is common at this point to want the "reward" of relaxing your discipline—and then comes the backslide! The painful fact remains that we must follow persistence with *more* persistence *and* vigilance. The old patterns of behavior have long, tough roots into our being, and many years of dominance. But if we continue to do what is good for us whether we feel like it or not, we build an utterly new foundation for the rest of our lives. There is a power in repetition that eventually realigns the patterns in our unconscious and allows us to become a different creature than we used to be.

My ongoing struggle with discipline has to do with my difficulty in working in a steady, organized, and focused way. I grew up in alcoholic chaos, so this is a real dragon for me. I tend to go to extremes, working too much or too little, and the sight of a pile of papers to file elicits emotions of hopelessness and feeling completely overwhelmed! But I keep working at this—my past successes assure me that I can indeed become an effective worker and a steady and successful businesswoman, despite my old conditioning. A few years from now I hope it will seem natural to be steady and orderly—another star on my chart!

TEN STEPS TO SELF DISCIPLINE

1. **Acknowledge the need to become more disciplined in how you live your life.**
   Crack through any denial operating about your out-of-control behavior. Make the distinction between discipline and punishment—discipline is an act of love. Deal with the emotions of rebelliousness.

2. **Seek inspiration.**
   Most of the world's great leaders and
   performers have had great personal discipline. Who are your heroes? Hang up their
   pictures—let their excellence call you forward
   to realize your own aims.

3. **Decide to become disciplined.**
   Choose an area where there is a crying need,
   and state your will to make change, with
   the help of your Higher Self. Say it aloud as
   a statement of your spiritual will. Here are
   some examples of a will statement: *I will
   become clean and organized. I will become
   honest with myself and others. I will finish what
   I start. I will take the time to cook a good meal.*

4. **Enlist support.**
   Choose new friends who demonstrate
   personal discipline and learn from them. Tell
   your current friends and family that you are
   making some difficult changes and that you
   want their support for your efforts. Talk to
   your Higher Self about it often.

5. **Release feelings of hopelessness.**
   Hopelessness will come up when you try to
   change long-standing patterns. Feel it, vent

some feelings about it, but don't believe it any more. Keep moving.

6. **Stay on track.**
Remind yourself every morning what your discipline is, and that it isn't optional. Do it. Post a copy of your will statement where you can see it. At night, review the day. Did you do what you needed to do today to produce long-term happiness? Check in with a friend about it at least once a week.

7. **Acknowledge your progress.**
Celebrate glimpses of health and accomplishment in your chosen area of discipline.

8. **Persist, persist, persist.**
Acquire a taste for repetition and good habits.

9. **Stabilize in your new mode.**
Give yourself time to get used to new behaviors, and remember that they're still new. It can take years to stabilize, but it's worth the effort.

10. **Be vigilant!**
Notice if you are relaxing your disciplines, and notice what happens to you and your life when you do. Remember the power of

repetition. Try not to be compulsive or rigid, but remember that too much relaxation isn't a treat for you—it is self-abandonment. You deserve the gifts that discipline will bring you.

"What is the greatest obstacle to spiritual growth?
Laziness ...."
- Shankaracharya

The Serenity Prayer

God, grant me the serenity
to accept the things I cannot change,
the courage to change the things I can,
and the wisdom to know the difference.

The Serenity Prayer, which has always been
an indispensable part of every Twelve Step gathering, has now taken its place as a classic modern
prayer. This prayer is a favorite for many people
because it contains the sum total of what spiritual
living is—a series of lessons about when to accept
life as it is and when to make changes for the
better. You can say this prayer thousands of times
and find it meaningful, because at any given
time we need to employ acceptance, courage, or
wisdom to feel peace of mind in the moment. For
many years on the spiritual journey we employ
these concepts self-consciously, but eventually we
become them in our beings.

In a way, this prayer is a global contemplation: the wisdom of the East and the West meets
here. The wisdom of the East teaches us to accept

life. *There is nowhere you have to go; it's all right here. Everything you see is equally One—the play of God's consciousness in a myriad of forms. Be at peace with what you are, here, now. Accept.* The wisdom of the West says the opposite. *You can be something more than what you are right now—strive for it! Life can be better! You can use your knowledge and will to make changes that advance evolution. There is no problem that cannot be solved and no creative innovation beyond your reach if you desire it. Courage!* It is the wisdom of the Whole that knows which wisdom must predominate now, though each is bound to the other as inseparable partners in the dance of creation through time.

The truth in the Serenity Prayer must be horse sense because my daughter understood it when she was only six. She gave me a fine lesson about it one night. I was in a stew about something that was not really my business, and she said, "Is there anything you can do about that?" I thought about it and replied that there wasn't. "Well then, Mom, I guess you'll just have to enjoy your own life," she told me. How did she figure that out at such a young age? There were thousands of adults all over the nation at that very moment struggling to fix other people's lives while feeling powerless to make any real changes in their own. I guess my daughter had not unlearned her basic human wisdom.

Those of us who grew up in dysfunctional homes need the basic human wisdom of the Serenity Prayer. We are out of balance at times because we do not truly accept life as it is or we are not using our wills to make changes we need to make to live better lives. We live trying lives. Several years ago my Inner Self said to me, *You must give up trying*. Trying what? I wondered. Before long I realized that *trying* has been my base line approach to life and that it is extremely stressful. I have been trying for so long—trying to win my dad's admiration, trying to save my family from alcoholic crisis, trying to be liked. Trying is the opposite of peace and success. We have to really accept life as it is, and use our skillful spiritual wills to open our lives to their fullest potential. Period. No more trying. It is the commitment to living this paradox fully that brings both serenity and excellence to a human life.

How do you gain acceptance of life as it is? My guess is that a healthy person in a healthy society gains this acceptance in the normal process of gaining maturity. You get to know and accept yourself, train your abilities, and employ them in service to others. You learn to accept your duties, accept others, accept the miracle of new life, and the mystery of death. You accept the challenges of your generation and its contribution to society. Acceptance grows in an incremental way, like the ring of new wood that the tree gains each year.

It's harder when you have to dig out of crippling childhood pain, but I think the years bring maturity and acceptance anyway, if we are open to them. Life itself teaches acceptance of life. Eventually we learn some things: *Nobody's perfect, especially me. I can't keep anybody—people change, die, move away. When a relationship is over, no matter how much love there is, it's over. I can't keep anything—things get lost, worn, outdated. Cars rust. Sometimes you get the flu. Some people aren't to be trusted. Governments are not necessarily just, and religious people aren't necessarily moral. It rains*

*on festivals and garage sales. Sunsets still the rest-
less mind. Luck and kindness come from unexpected
sources—it's best to receive them! I can't take away
another person's suffering or their responsibilities.
This has all happened before and it will all happen
again ....*

With increasing maturity, acceptance is no
longer a thought or process; it is a relaxed, open
state of being. It is the state of being empty and
full simultaneously, and established in the Now.
A person living in this graceful state of acceptance
is a supporter of the positive potential in every
moment, for everyone.

The free and powerful human beings—
enlightened masters—live in this manner. These
saints have become so established in acceptance
of life as it is that they are radiant lights of peace,
love, and joy, regardless of environment or
circumstance. And yet the will of their personality
is so powerfully aligned with the Divine Will,
that miraculous things are accomplished through
them all the time, with no effort. No trying! They
choose to enhance the liberation of other people
with calm detachment. They are able to see

perfection in imperfection! This is the fantastic human potential contained in seedling form in the Serenity Prayer.

A comic I once saw put the case for accepting life as it is in this way: "The Universe, in fact, is God's seventh grade science experiment. He only got a 'C' on it." Isn't that great? With this perspective we can see that maybe even God Himself is evolving, and we're all a part of it. Let's truly accept the things we cannot change, and change the things we can, with the wisdom to know the difference.

Keep coming back! It works if you work it.
- Twelve Step slogan

CREATE YOUR REALITY?

Some people say that it's the biggest turning point in human thought since the Copernican Revolution. Since the early 1980s, large numbers of people have embraced the idea that the reality each of us experiences is a projection of the beliefs in our own mind, and that we have some say about what that reality will be. We are not victims of anything, we hear. It's the secret in *The Secret:* We can decide how we want life to be, and create it that way—from our thoughts! The sky's the limit!

I engage this notion personally as a partial truth, and with mixed emotions. On one hand, I agree. It's an empowering idea that encourages us to take full responsibility for our lives, to the extent that we can. It's the end of a victim mind-set and the beginning of claiming our full spiritual identity. It also invites us into the realm of all possibility. On the other hand, I've seen people buy this, try it, and fail at it so quickly that they feel ashamed of their lives as they are, because they now believe that there shouldn't be

anything we can't create—there shouldn't be any
limits to our possibilities. They're embarrassed
and discouraged because they think they *should*
be creating a more attractive reality than they can
show their friends at this moment. They *should*
have more *control* over things than they do.

I've made it my personal job to say "Yes,
but—" about Create Your Reality, and have inves-
tigated some of the fine print. I know it isn't cool
to say "can't" in these days of limitless possibility,
but someone's got to do it. If you subscribe to this
otherwise fine paradigm, I now present Mary's
Mindful Maxims as a consumer warning.

MINDFUL MAXIMS FOR CREATING YOUR REALITY

1. **You can't create what you can't receive.**
   Usually, you have to also do a hefty piece of
   emotional work when you start to seriously
   change your life from the level of your mind.
   If you don't truly feel deserving enough to
   have a kind mate or a new car, you won't
   get them until at least some of your toes are
   firmly planted on the new ground of knowing

that you are worthy of them. You might have to do some personal healing of childhood issues in order to get that attitude in place.

2. **You can't have a new attitude by next week.** You can start today, and persist through next week, but you need to stick with it for much longer than that before your attitude change reaches deep enough to change your outer experiences. You have to passionately live your new attitude for at least six to nine months to get around the corner from the old to the new.

3. **You can't create a new reality from your conscious mind if you still carry an old belief buried in your unconscious.** Sometimes you have to be a detective to discern what negative belief must be operating to create a repetitive unhappy reality. It could be from a buried childhood event or a past life. Hypnosis, dream work, or a consultation with a mental health professional may help you dig it out and look at it. Then you can change it.

4. **You can't go from rags to riches overnight.** It usually takes years, even decades. It is very

unlikely that you will be lifted from poverty with a lottery ticket, or be asked to appear on a big-money game show. Upgrading your economic reality goes in steps and stages—you might have to go to school next, or plan some other practical strategy for raising your income. You will have to keep healing into greater self-esteem and personal power to be able to attract greater financial opportunities.

5. **You can't move on to new situations until you have completely embraced and participated in the one you are in.**
This present situation is also your creation. What is here? Have you brought as much love and intelligence to it as you can? Have you embraced the spiritual learning inherent in this current opportunity? It's like school—you need to complete your current course work before you enroll in the next level of learning.

6. **You can't create something that is incorrect for your personal spiritual journey.**
You already created this life, theoretically, to learn and accomplish certain things. You can't completely change the program half way through.

7. **You can do anything,
   but you can't do it without God's help.**

8. **God will help, but God won't do it for you.**

9. **Maybe you can have it all, but you can't
   have it all at the same time.**

   Life is a game, some people say, but every
   game has rules and limits that define what
   the challenge is. On Earth our challenge
   is a friendly struggle between desire and
   surrender, time limits and limitless possibility.
   That's why reincarnation makes practical
   sense in most religious systems. There are so
   many ways of playing this game that once
   isn't enough to exhaust our interest in it.

10. **Accept your limits.**

    Limits give shape to your life. You came to
    Earth because you desired to experience some
    things. You poured your limitlessness into a
    singular form that is known as *you,* so that
    you could drink of life and be enjoyed by life.
    Maybe this is it! Be okay as you, limits and
    all. Then go for it!

If you have built castles in the air,
your work need not be lost;
that is where they should be.
Now put the foundations under them.
- Henry David Thoreau

Giving and Receiving

The ability to genuinely give and receive is a challenge for many of us. This is especially true if we grew up in environments that were painfully out of balance in terms of healthy giving and receiving. Some people learned to give-give-give as a way of feeling valued and important in some way. Others learned to take everything they could get—more than their share—in an attempt to fill a gaping hole inside. As adults, these people often get into relationships with each other and engage in a frustrating dance of immature love that ends in alienation, guilt, and blame. In fact, both people bear the same wound. It is the wound of the needy child.

Very few people in our world get all of their childhood needs met. We are all part of the largest dysfunctional family in the world—the human race! Children need to be thoughtfully raised, protected, and nourished by a centered pair of grown-ups with the support of extended family and community. They need to be seen and appreciated for who they are, and guided into unfolding their potential. In many families, this is not the case, and you're lucky if you get a modicum of protection and "three hots and a cot"—some don't even get that.

If our needs are not met as children, we become perpetually needy inside. As adults we may adapt to this painful unmet need by becoming reckless givers with an exaggerated sense of responsibility toward others and an inability to receive what we need, even if it is staring us right in the face. Or we may be selfish and self-absorbed, unable to respond to the needs of others without feeling resentful and taken advantage of. We may experience both of these attitudes in different areas of our lives.

Being human means having needs and having to meet the needs of others. There is no way around it. A whole person is one who is able to give and receive comfortably and appropriately. It's like breathing. You can't just breathe out constantly without taking air in again. You'll die. You can't just take in the air and withhold your carbon dioxide from the environment. You have to give it back. A healthy human is meant to be constantly giving and receiving in an easy steady rhythm, exactly like breathing. Breathe in, breathe out. Breathe in, breathe out. Receive, give. Receive, give. Simple. Sometimes, however, the simplicity of this basic function must be regained by steady self-healing.

It is human nature to yearn towards wholeness. Even when you are choosing the wrong people and situations and replaying your original wounds, you are actually attempting to heal yourself. Subconsciously you choose people and situations that resemble your family. You think, *If I only try hard, I can make this person change, and then they will meet my needs.* As you probably know, it never works that way. You cannot successfully fill a frozen need of the past by controlling someone in the present. You can never do it right enough, and they will tire of you and leave you with your gaping hole and a fresh wound to lick.

To heal the needy child within, you need to have your face turned continuously to the nourishing presence of the Higher Self. You can accept God as Mother and Father, and entrust your needs once again to a parent who won't let you down. This Spirit is enormously talented at providing you with people and circumstances to steadily heal your wound, meet your need, and bring you into balance. It *wants* to help you move into greater harmony! You just need to be willing to receive what is coming to you, and give what life is asking you to give.

Some people are afraid to receive. They feel guilty, afraid they are not deserving of something good, especially when they haven't asked for it. Or they fear they are depriving someone else by accepting something they need. Some people are afraid to receive because they believe they will become vulnerable to another's manipulation, or be "in debt" to the person giving. It takes a balanced understanding and good self-esteem to be able to receive the goodness Life is capable of giving us. This understanding and self-esteem can be gained in steady increments as soon as one is willing to *s-t-r-e-t-c-h* open to it a bit at a time. We are each capable of expanding our ability to receive and enjoy life's goodness.

It takes a certain amount of trust and

vulnerability to receive good things—you have to be willing to be open to the unexpected. You may need to acknowledge that someone else really sees you and your need and cares enough about you to serve that need, freely.

I have a neighbor who is a single mother of seven kids, all living at the poverty line. Every time she sees me she tells me how exhausted she is. And yet when I sincerely offer her some kind of help she refuses it. I finally realized that she is unwilling to be vulnerable to me and my caring. She wants to struggle along with what is familiar and complain about it because she doesn't want to open her heart to unexpected human compassion. Why? Maybe she'll cry.

Sometimes you need to cry in order to receive. You need to feel and release old pain instead of running from it and remaining in a rut. People who are more interested in transformation than in total control will walk forward into new and unfamiliar realms like intimacy and happiness, even if they are filled with uncertainty because these things are so new. The ability to genuinely give also requires some good understanding of when it's right to do so. At times you have experienced the sweet exhilaration and openness of true giving, and at other times when you gave you felt drained or resentful afterwards. What is the difference? You may have felt drained for one of these reasons:

- You were giving with a motive and an attachment to a certain outcome or response from the other person. This is *not* giving, it is manipulation!
- You were giving to someone who was *taking*, but not able to *receive*. Think about that one for a while.
- You were giving beyond what was really practical for you to do. Our time, energy, and resources are valuable, and the ability to exercise a certain amount of positive control over them is necessary.

One day you may be sitting in a café and an acquaintance sits down to tell you her problems. It is practical for you to lend a helping ear, and you choose to do that. Giving and receiving take place and you both feel good about the encounter. If, however, your purpose in sitting there is to be alone with your own thoughts, and this person sits down and begins to talk, you cannot really give to her. You need to be true to your own intentions and inform her in an open-hearted way that you really don't want to talk to anyone right now. Your honesty is the best gift to both of you at that moment. Say "no" to that person as though you are handing them a gift.

There are times when we are able to stretch our capacity for giving way beyond our previous practical limits. Special situations can call forth from within us a wellspring of love and service, and the perception that all giving is receiving, for there is only one Self that is both the servant and the recipient of that same love. This is the highest perception, and one that a serious spiritual seeker will eventually attain and keep. Once Mother Teresa was asked, "How could you have person-ally picked up thousands of dying bodies from the streets of Calcutta?" She replied, "I have only lifted One."

"The Creator gave us the Sun, our elder brother.
It is his duty to give us warmth, and to nourish
the life-giving foods that are planted on Earth.
And as we see, the Sun came up this morning,
and shines on us, keeping us warm.
He's doing his duty, and for this we are very grateful.
So let us all put our minds together as one,
and thank the Sun for still performing his duty.
And let our minds be that way."
- from a Thanksgiving speech, Onondaga elder

"For it is in giving that we receive."
- prayer of St. Francis

Everything's Not Under Control

"You're so controlling!" I can't tell you how many times over the last twenty years I have heard my husband exclaim this in a moment of exasperation. I confess: I resemble this remark. I'm one of those people who are notorious for trying to control people and things in their environment.

My poor husband is often at the wrong end of my controlling behavior. I want to monitor how much he works, how much TV he watches, and how he does his job as a father. He *should* be paying more attention to *me*. I also want to control my daughter—what she eats and what she wears. She *must* be healthy and socially appropriate. I don't want to stop there, though. I think tomorrow I'll tackle the drug pushers, the AMA, and the President, and make them all behave themselves. Why, I don't know why God doesn't hand over the keys to running the Universe right now! I'd do a heck of a job, and consult with Him only rarely, just to keep in touch.

Doesn't reading this make you tense? I must be tense whenever I am controlling. It seems to me that the need to feel in control of everything is a byproduct of an essential lack of trust in life. When I am controlling, I am trying to make everything be "all right" because I don't know and trust that everything really *is* all right. Perhaps it would be better if I attempt to go to a new level of faith and trust in my Higher Power. This means coming into a healthy relationship with "control."

The correct exercise of control is such a human dilemma. As a species, humans love control! We want to control our environment, our physical and emotional safety, our financial security, our self-image. We tend to want to control others or be controlled by them. We create roles, habits, rules, and personal and political systems out of the need to control. We're good at this, and a lot of it is necessary to establish a baseline of order and a healthy status quo. And yet it is this same passion for control that gets us into trouble—as individuals and as a species. If we do not exercise wisdom, control can easily become addiction, tyranny, and repression. Then we find ourselves rebelling from excessive control with a cry of *Freedom!* and we take refuge in creative chaos. Eventually the need for structure reemerges, if we are serious about manifesting our ideas in the world around us.

If you are serious about discovering and fulfilling your purpose, you must come into a right relationship with control on every level of your being: physical, emotional, mental, and spiritual. The point of having *some* control over your world is to have a foundation upon which to dance with life's spontaneity. Life's creative unpredictability is both unsettling and delicious. We really have no ultimate control over most of it. But we can trust life anyway if we come into a correct relationship with control on an emotional level. There's really nothing you can't handle as long as you can have your feelings about it, and share them with others. People, jobs, and homes will come and go in your life, bringing up a lot of feelings. Everyone has their own cache of buried pain awaiting to erupt to the surface for healing. Our organism is always yearning toward health and wholeness, and our life situations will repeat the drama of our early wounds until we fully feel and heal them.

One of the most common human problems is the desire to control and repress the experience of painful emotions. If you spend your time and money on substances or projects designed to prevent you from feeling painful old emotions, you will remain on a limited track with your life, and your mind and body will become more rigid and less adaptable as you age. But if you realize that your pain is a gift, and if you are determined to trust Life, you will use your time and resources to feel your pain and heal from it instead of avoiding it with an addiction. There are, however, some people who need to exert more control over their feeling nature because they are awash in emotion. They need to learn to contain their feelings, and to discipline themselves to bring focus to their personality.

There is one power you always have that no one can ever take away from you—and that is the power to take a point of view. This is the correct way to have control on a mental level. We cannot force Life to unfold according to our demands. What we *can* do is definitively release our previous expectations of life, and turn our hearts and our will to loving it as it is now. We can learn to accept that in some inexplicable way, all is well—even when things are *not* going as we expected. This is an empowering point of view that you can adopt in any circumstance, because it keeps you from slipping into the sloppy stance of a victim.

I met a woman once who really understands this. She was so alive and excited about her journey and the mysterious, inevitable unfolding of God's plan for her life. She had just suddenly lost her job of eighteen years in a company reorganization. Instead of blaming her superiors as they laid her off, she could hardly keep from smiling and exulting in the wonderful surprise God must have in store for her to move her along so abruptly!

I have been thinking that the current climate of insecurity most people have about their jobs is really a blessing in disguise. Now that previously stable companies have merged and disappeared and reincarnated all over the place, masses of people have been forced to abandon their belief in an external source of security. They are turning to inner resources of serenity amid a sea of change, and starting to listen to spiritual impulses for new direction in their lives. Security is and always has been a very temporal thing, subject to change. Serenity amid the rise and fall of the endless things in life that are beyond our control is a much more precious commodity—and we can always choose it and have it. *This* is self-control.

The challenge for self-control on the spiritual level is being willing to let go of the known, and follow our spiritual impulses. This is different than the scattered, uninformed impulsiveness of a childish person who is afraid to think through consequences. It is different from compulsion, which is rigid, repetitive, and familiar. Our inner being is constantly communicating to us its desire and direction through spontaneous impulses.

These impulses come to us in a flash in our mind's eye, or a little voice that says, *"Why don't you ...?"* Sometimes your hand reaches out to someone you hardly know and you touch them with compassion. When we act on divine impulse there is a sense of stepping across the gap of the unknown into a new realm. Like a mountain climber in the crystalline air of the present moment, you have a quiet mind and relaxed concentration. For a moment, we suspend judgment and concerns about outcome, and *follow,* with trust and detachment. It is this willingness to walk through the beckoning doorway of possibility that brings adventure to life, and opens us to receive from God more than we can imagine creating ourselves. Yet it is the control we skillfully employ in our life that enables us to contain this goodness, and continue strengthening the foundation to hold more.

> *"Life is what happens to you while you're*
> *busy making other plans."*
> *- John Lennon*

LIVING IN CONTENTMENT

I've got a problem. What will I do? I got into this journey of self-healing many years ago because I observed that my life was a wreck and I was a pain in the neck for people I wanted to be close to. I worked hard on understanding some issues that painfully limited me, and I've made a lot of changes. I am now trustworthy to myself and others, and have even accomplished some worthy goals and gained respect in my community. My problem is this: my journey has brought me to the borders of an unfamiliar country: Contentment.

I've heard about this country, but long ago in my chaotic state I decided it must be a dangerous place, one to be avoided. Isn't it bland, boring, and mind-numbing there? Doesn't it seduce one to forget one's responsibility to solve the world's problems? Won't I lose my passion, my intensity, and my identity as a heroic fighter who is *trying* to beat unbeatable odds? Besides, my ancestors came from the country of Struggle, and who am I to leave my heritage and take up alien residence in the land of Peace and Plenty?

Being content is a tough aesthetic choice I am making in my life. If there was a painting of the psychological landscape of my old world view it would look like a masterpiece sprung from the brush of the American painter Jackson Pollack. Chaos swirls amid intensity of color and movement ... murky hints of evil and destruction ... shock and struggle screech rebelliously from the canvas—*Life! Freedom!* Whew. Pretty interesting, but I think it's too hard to live there for long.

I turn to the painting of the landscape now beckoning to me. It looks like it's painted by Paul Cezanne. Quiet hills and trees have small homes nestling cozily among them in perfect balance. Soft tones describe a land watered with calm rivers of meaning and interconnection with others. It is not without interest—look! Suddenly a large swan flaps upward to the sky from the inlet where it was just hidden. Can I choose this peaceful valley of contentment? Not yet. I need to understand more about contentment before I do.

One thing I'm quite sure of is that the experience of contentment within a situation has little to do with the *con*tent of the situation. Contentment is an attitude, a choice of where I will focus my attention. A situation can change completely, and you can remain just as unhappy, if you have an attitude of discontent. I learned this by going on vacation.

For many years, my experience of summer in the inner city where I live was my favorite scenario of self-torture and discontent. If I indulge it, I can easily chafe and moan about living in the middle of the hot urban crush of South Minneapolis instead of a civilized upper middle-class neighborhood like a few of my siblings do. I first moved onto this block in 1988 when a Buddhist client of mine who was relieving herself of all worldly possessions practically *threw* this house at me for nothing. It was a good opportunity because there I was with a newly disabled husband, my struggling young entrepre-neurial business, and no financial resources to buy a house another way.

We moved into this 1910 charmer without much supporting data that it was a good idea. I figured if we didn't like it, we could move again in a few years. Before long I found myself grimly referring to my city block as "Little Bombay." Here, there was an unfairly high concentration of people who had no manners, no mufflers, no fathers, or no scruples. Garbage and broken glass littered the street, and day and night there was a cacophony of barking dogs, honking horns, drunken fights and swearing children. This offended my preference for beauty and quiet. I wanted to get the hell out of there, but couldn't.

One summer I thought I would be able to bear it if I went to the quiet Wisconsin woods for two weeks. I arranged a cabin-on-a-lake-at-a-small-family-resort vacation, and comforted myself all summer by glancing at the last two weeks of August outlined in marker on the kitchen calendar. At last the great day came, and we launched our escape.

Well, it was quiet. But the cabin was dark, smelly and claustrophobic. There were tacky pictures on all the walls. The tap water was golden brown. They charged us extra for linen. It rained for two days and then remained cloudy and muggy for a few more. There were flies and mosquitoes in the air and a rumor of leeches in the lake. During the long indoor days my daughter repetitively played her Sesame Street tape or my husband repetitively played Indian raga music.

I began to thrash and writhe in discontent! I myself became a toxic pollutant in our small cabin environment, and my husband and daughter sought refuge in solitaire and other children's families. After several days of this I decided to salvage the remnants of my self-respect, and discipline myself into a better attitude. It wasn't easy, but the other choice appeared to be another week of misery and my increasing unpopularity with my family.

I sat down with a notebook and made a list of things I would have preferred about this vacation environment. (Sweet clean water ... airy rooms ... sunny days ... free sheets, etc.) I allowed myself to fully savor each preference while telling myself that I would no longer *expect* these things. My expectations and attachments were causing me to suffer. Then I heaved a big sigh and wrote the reasons why being there was a gift and a blessing. I listed everything positive that had occurred there so far, and without trying very hard, my plus list outweighed the minus two to one. I acknowledged gratitude for these things, and shifted my focus of attention for the rest of the week. We all had a good time.

Every circumstance we find ourselves in has a front and a back side to it, and our experience of contentment lies in our ability to choose the focus of our attention. Some people say that contentment is "wanting what you have." I agree with that, and in addition I say that in any given situation, some goal of mine is being fulfilled. I am not a victim of anything! I may not perceive that I am getting what I need because I have both short-term and long-term goals in operation. There are times when some of them are on "hold" while others are getting their due. I think the art of contentment lies in the ability to see how I am reaping what I have asked for.

A number of years ago I earnestly asked God to give me complete and unshakable self-esteem. I heard an inner Voice say, "Fine. You've got it. It will take you five years to attain that goal." And sure enough, over the next five years I found myself in situations that directly nurtured my self-esteem or challenged it to the roots. In the more difficult scenarios, I chose to see that this was an answer to my prayer and an opportunity to gain on my goal.

In the case of my stressful urban environment, I did not meet my short-term goal of getting a good night's sleep all summer. But I did meet my short-term goal of living extremely cheaply so I didn't have to work long hours while I brought up my two children. I've had lots of family and leisure time that I wouldn't have had if I were struggling to make a large mortgage payment as a single breadwinner. I was also forced to work on some important long-term spiritual goals: cultivating *inner* peace, and developing enough humility to see God in all persons equally. If I choose to remember that the attainment of equality consciousness is a serious goal of mine, I see this city block as exactly the best learning laboratory to achieve that golden goal. Between work and home, I get to socialize with CEO's, university vice presidents and welfare moms all on the same day. Just what I asked for, I guess.

LIVING IN CONTENTMENT

1. **The experience of healthy discontent** arises because we have some practical or spiritual needs that must be met.

2. **We create goals** to meet those needs and observe contentedly the manner in which the goals are being realized.

3. **We practice realism** about the impermanence and unpredictability of life, and the willingness to let go of each and every one of these desires or attainments when it is time.

I once bitterly cried out to God about how betrayed I felt because all the people I love could be taken away from me through death or some other change. I have no control around that loss and pain. I heard that inner Voice say, *I haven't let you down. I never told you that you could keep anybody. That's not part of the deal here.* Oh.

Everything is impermanent. Jobs, homes, people, your body. It is as if each of these things is a mere container that will only hold what you fill it with—love or fear. The containers are continuously created and maintained for a while. Then they either gently deteriorate or abruptly break apart. Imagine! What if you approached your whole life with the delight and detachment with which you sit in the sun and blow soap bubbles from a toy wand! When you set out to blow bubbles you fully expect them to be impermanent, yet you do it anyway. You want to see how many you can make at once, how big they can be, how long they can last, and in what manner they will eventually break. You treasure each unique rainbow-streaked sphere for as long as it lasts, confident that there will always be more for as long as you choose to play.

This is my picture of contentment. I will not choose the painting of the quiet valley by Cezanne. There could always be bulldozers in the future. I will choose a painting by Maxfield Parrish that shows a sweet-faced person sitting on a mountain height blowing bubbles into the air.

That person is an innocent, comfortably vulnerable to life. Perhaps it takes a certain amount of deliberate innocence to live a life of contentment these days. The lofty perch gives them just the right perspective on things. Face to face with the Creator, the contented person blows beautiful delicate creations that grace the world for a while and then pass on their way—as the Creator does with each one of us.

Don't worry!
Whatever is supposed to happen will happen —
it never fails!
Face everything contentedly
while absorbing your mind in God.
- Lalleshwari

A WILD TRUST

"I don't know what I *need!*" I cried out
in exasperation one day. I was facing one of the
greatest dilemmas a person with low self-esteem
can face: a positive opportunity. I had just
received a respectable bundle of money from a
five-year-long court battle that finally resolved,
and now I had some resources to make choices
above and beyond the status quo and the month-
to-month bills. Since childhood I was acclimated
to struggle, and the arrival of an opportunity
for choice and ease was so foreign that it was
stressful. Strangely, it made me depressed.

"I know what you need," one of my friends
suggested confidently. "Just trust me on this."

A week later I was on my way to a five-day
treatment center for the family members of alcoholics. On the first day, my counselor said a few
simple things that uncorked a river of tears that
flowed without interruption for most of the time
I was there. I allowed myself to be herded along
from group to group, from morning to night,
and I learned to see my crisis orientation as a

fallout effect of my father's disease. I grieved the loss of childhood, and the physical and emotional neglect I experienced as a child. By the end of the program a significant change had taken place: I went home with a small but sturdy understanding that I am a worthy person who deserves to have what she needs.

But what was that? Should I move out of the inner city to a quieter neighborhood? Take that trip to Ireland? Go to art school? I didn't know. I started by looking at different neighborhoods. I looked for a few months, but always found myself saying, "It's just not quiet enough to warrant the trouble of moving, and there aren't enough trees." Was I being a perfectionist? Even the premier neighborhoods in my city were not quiet enough or pretty enough for me.

One day my best friend called up and said, "Let's go to the meditation program tonight. I feel really drawn to it so I bet it'll be a good one." We went and it was nice—nothing stellar. But after the program I spoke to a woman about my house search and she said, "I don't know why I'm telling you this, but there is this piece of land that I know of, and the owner needs to sell it. He might even already have sold it to the government, but I just think you should go see it."

"What the heck," I thought. "It's May. A beautiful time for a field trip."

So my husband Fred and I followed the lead, and made arrangements to see the land, even though the owner thought the government was going to buy it soon. The land was located on the St. Croix River, in an area almost completely surrounded by forest and a protected wild river country. We had been told that there were only seven permanent dwellings in a ten-mile radius. We left the pavement and the farms behind and crunched for miles down a long gravel road. As we passed a field, a black shape caught my attention. It wasn't a cow.

"Fred, stop!" I cried, "That's a bear!"

We stopped the car. The bear ambled through the sunny field right towards us, his blue-black fur gleaming with health. He was the spirit of relaxation itself, and his whole manner communicated the ease of a wild thing who feels safe in his habitat. He was mellow. Then he saw us, and loped away into the brush.

"A bear! A *bear*!" I was beside myself with simple, mindless joy. My whole being was energized. I remembered what a friend of mine predicted for me during our Spring Equinox meditation. *You are going to meet a wild animal this year, and it's going to awaken a part of you that you have forgotten about. It's going to change your life.* I couldn't imagine what she meant then, but I could feel a big change happening now. When we got to the property and pulled into the long driveway, Fred said, "I have the strangest feeling that I'm coming home."

We toured the house and the forty acres, accompanied by Dan, the son of Dick, the owner. In a way, the visual appearance of the land was unremarkable; the forest was kind of bare and scruffy because the sandy soil can only support jack pines, birches, and oaks. Things grow slowly there, and fall down if they get too big. This pine barrens forest and grassland area had almost a desert quality. But there was something remark-able, something shimmering within every blade of grass on the property. This place was saturated with the palpable feeling of love. The garden, the birdhouses on trees far and near, the tubs of water placed strategically for the deer to drink from—all spoke of the owner's deep appreciation for nature. And beneath and beyond his relationship with it, the place was infused with wildness.

As we entered a large field under the open sky, I was embarrassed to find myself nodding off into a trance while the three of us were standing there talking. I excused myself before it was too noticeable and went off to sit alone for a while in the middle of the field. I went into a deep meditation there, the likes of which I have only experienced a few times, in very holy places. In utter silence, I could sense the still heart of the Earth beneath me, and I could feel her consciousness breathing freely from her center to the outer stratosphere. "Here," I thought, "she still breathes deeply—unencumbered by cement and human inventions."

All potential obstacles melted before us, and upon their son Dan's advice, Dick and his wife Viola decided that Fred and I should be the next stewards of their beloved land. They withdrew the deal from the government. When I met Dick and Viola for the first time at the bank closing, I had every intention of proceeding with dignity, but instead I burst into uncontrollable tears of happiness right there in the bank lobby. "There, there," Viola said, patting me and offering me a Kleenex. "You're going to have many wonderful years there, just like we did."

She held my hand in her wrinkled one as I quietly snuffled and hiccupped over all the papers the banker passed around the table. It was a four-hankie signing, and everyone but the banker was moist by the time we were done. We went out to lunch to celebrate, and I was touched to see how much this land meant to Dick. He tried to tell us so many things about it, but his sentences trailed off in confusion, his mind crippled by the stroke that had forced him to leave the land and move to town near his children. "I used to be so smart, so strong. I could do anything. I'm just a dunce now! I don't like who I am anymore." "Oh, Dick," Viola said, "Now don't talk like that." "I see that you really hate these limitations," I said.

"I don't blame you for feeling like you do."

Six days later, Dick died. He succumbed quickly to a heart condition that had not been previously diagnosed. His family had a small service in his home, and Fred and I were the only people who were not immediate family who were invited. Looking around the crowded living room, I had the eerie feeling that I already knew every one of these people. Even though the Fundamentalist service was different than my own beliefs, there was a sense that I was among kindred spirits. They embraced Fred, my daughter Tara, and me as part of their own. I stood up during the speaking part of the service and thanked all of them for bringing so much love to the land at their family gatherings over the years. When I invited them all to walk there any time they wished, the entire group heaved a collective sigh of relief. They lost Dick, but they wouldn't have to lose the land, too.

During the course of the evening everyone came up to us one by one to tell us their favorite stories ... the time the bear came to the window ... the time Mother saw the black snake and made the neighbor move it and he fainted afterwards, the deer who brought her new fawns to show Dick because he was her friend ... the night they saw the UFO—what else could it have been ...? I collected their stories in my heart like the wild strawberries they all gathered in baskets in the spring when they were children. My child and her friends will gather them now.

We lingered outside in the sunset when it was time to go, reluctant to dissolve this experience of unexpected community. Suddenly a large monarch butterfly flew from the doorway of the house, right between my head and Fred's, beating a straight path for the horizon. It flew with a strength and focus that seemed uncharacteristic of a butterfly.

"Fred, that was Dick!" I knew it was his spirit signaling a joyous farewell. I could sense the completion of this passage of land, and the freedom he enjoyed from dropping his limited body.

My land has been my healer. Season by season, year after year—it nurtures a new trust in life that is growing in my heart. For now, we straddle two worlds, inner city and remote country. It is a perfect balance. I feel safe there, in a place that is so silent you can hear the wind coming to you long before it reaches your face. We have seen eagles, hawks, porcupines, beavers, deer, all sorts of birds, a few snakes, and two more big black bears. The sight of a wild creature living in its own way fills me with excitement that lasts for days. I can't explain the joy I feel when I am walking in the scruffy woods and I stumble upon a hole in the sand that is obviously a doorway to someone's home. Whose? Fox? Badger? I must remember these footprints, and look them up ....

One weekend Fred was on the land by himself, and I stayed in the city. He told me that he found himself being guided from place to place around the forty acres, and at each place he found traces of Dick's unfinished odds and ends. "It's just uncanny," he said. "It's like he's here showing me around."

That night I dreamed peacefully of Fred walking and working the land, a large monarch butterfly resting on his forehead.

"In wildness is the preservation of the world."
- Henry David Thoreau

DEVELOP YOUR INTUITION

I don't know. It's just a gut-level feeling. Just a hunch. Only women's intuition.

It's funny how deprecating we are about that quiet knowing that comes right out of our souls. That's what intuition is—the prompting of our soul to go toward the paths that will bring us the most goodness in our lives. It speaks to us in different ways. To some people it is the "still, small voice within." To others, it comes as a picture in the mind in either the waking state or the dream state. It can be a gut-level feeling, a sense of emotional comfort or discomfort. It flows through sensitive and skillful touch, and also has the ability to move through the world with luck and good timing. It is the flash of full-blown *knowing* that drops suddenly into our consciousness from out of the blue, bringing information or inspiration.

Unfortunately, most of us repress the strength of intuition, and insist that it be subordinate to the logical mind. We regard intuition as an unsettling, possibly embarrassing second cousin to the functions of logic, control, and linear thinking that we have been trained to rely on. We ignore intuition's polite suggestions for so long that it either atrophies into total silence or finds loud dramatic ways of getting through to us. Sometimes we don't listen to what we know until our life goes off the road in some messy crisis that forces us to give up our reliance to the logical "shoulds" in our minds.

The biggest blocks to using intuition successfully are fear and doubt. This is an historical problem. Intuition, like other aspects of the feminine psyche, has been delegated to the basement by the two major belief-making machines in Western culture—religion and science. In its darkest days, the Christian church waged a centuries-long campaign against the feminine. The Burning Times in Europe consumed the bodies of up to nine million women who were accused of the crime of witchcraft. A woman could be accused of being a witch if she were an herbalist, a midwife, or a psychic, careers that had long held honor in the prior Goddess-based religion. She was suspect if she was sexually attractive or a bit too "uppity." People were now expected to be obedient to the Church hierarchy and go to priests for mediation with God. No more listening to your own inner voices—they were most likely evil, the prompting of Satan. The Church established a deep climate of fear that we still carry in our collective subconscious mind. On a subconscious level, we are afraid to listen to our inner voices because they might be evil. We are caught in our own doubt about our basic goodness, and our fear of getting in trouble if we seem abnormal in any way.

The culture of scientific materialism grew up in reaction to this crazed church. Early scientists saw the need for a discipline of knowledge that could not be polluted by superstition, politics, or ungrounded mysticism. Science will allow only what can be seen, measured, counted, predicted, and proven. "Truth" is what can be demonstrated in controlled, repeatable experiments. This is fine and necessary in certain spheres, but the scientific method can't address all that makes a human life worth living. How could you prove a poem? Why should you measure a dance? Predict unconditional love? Ridiculous. And yet, somehow we let the religion of scientific materialism run our lives too. We are afraid of being thought "crazy" if we make decisions that do not lie within the bulging bell curve of "normal." We are afraid to step out of the linear march of our culture's conditioning to follow the call of the heart into some different experiences. We remain caged in self-doubt.

Your intuition is trying to show you only one thing all of the time: how to be happy as you. It's there to make life easier. Your intuition will help you understand and unfold your purpose here, and solve everyday problems. It needs to be reinstated on the throne next to the logical mind, where they can work as partners. Your intuition receives vision for a life direction that will make you happy and will use your unique nature to the fullest. Your planning mind makes a strategy. But it can't make an airtight strategy, because there are always unknowns. Your intuition works through these unknowns, bringing ideas and resources into play right in the present moment. Your logical mind organizes information; it balances your checkbook. Your intuition balances your life. It tells you about health needs, connects you with good friends, and helps you with timing. It leads you into situations that elicit joy. Together the intuition and the logical mind create a fulfilling and effective life.

Intuition operates in large and small ways. A number of years ago my intuition showed me in a dream that I needed to relocate to a different city as soon as possible. My logical mind was appalled and embarrassed—I had no reason to go there, and I had school to finish in my hometown. I had a lot of friends and family who would be sad and mystified at my move. But it was a strong feeling, so I did it. I met my beloved husband in a grocery store on my first venture into town. We fell in love instantly. And my health improved dramatically. I had been sick with a variety of complaints for almost two years. Now I discovered that I had been a creature at odds with my old environment, and I was more relaxed and healthy in my new location.

My intuition helps me with smaller challenges too. While driving around on errands, my little voice said, *Go home right now!* My logical mind told me I needed to go to the store first. *Really, right now! Go home.* My logical mind whined as I turned toward home, prematurely as far as it was concerned. As I entered my front door, the phone was ringing. It was a person I had tried to get in touch with unsuccessfully for a number of days. We made a quick little transaction that eased my current work project, and I went out again, smiling.

DEVELOP YOUR INTUITION

1. **Acknowledge that it's there.**
   Even if it is atrophied from disuse, your intuition can be awakened and brought into your life. Talk to it. Say, "Hi, I know you're there. I'd like you to be working in my life. Please become active so I can be happy and purposeful."

2. **Notice how your intuition speaks to you.**
   Do you hear a little voice, almost like the rest of your thoughts, but not quite? Do you see pictures in your mind? Do you *know* things,

but doubt that you know them because you don't have actual "proof"? Does your body give you cues about whether certain people are trustworthy? Discover which of these modes is strongest, and focus on that mode.

3. **Take some risks.**
   Start small, but start now to follow those little hunches instead of your conditioned brain. See where your own energy *wants* to go, not where you think it *should* go. Do some things because it feels right, not because it makes sense. Follow the "spiritual impulse."

4. **Trial and error.**
   Good discrimination between the intuitive mind and the conditioned mind takes time and practice. Don't doubt everything just because sometimes you're wrong. *Decide* to be accurate with intuition, and keep practicing.

5. **Become willing to flow more in your life.**
   Let your life be easier. Cultivate an appetite for synchronicity and surprise. Being in control all the time is exhausting and unimaginative. Let the creativity of the Universe into your life and enjoy it!

(now the ears of my ears awake and
the eyes of my eyes are opened)
- e.e. cummings

HUMILITY

"Blessed are the meek,
for they shall inherit the Earth."
- Jesus

A counselor of mine once told me that she saw me as a person with a great deal of power and energy that I was scattering to the winds with my erratic undisciplined behavior. She asked me why I was afraid to have power. I replied that I had been taught by my religious upbringing that I should be humble and not call attention to myself or ask for too much for myself. She looked at me and asked, "But what does humility really mean to *you?*" To my surprise my voice answered from an inner knowing: "Humility is taking one's rightful place in the Universe." I'm still in the process of trying to fully understand what that means.

Humility has really gotten a bad rap. Generally, people think of humility as taking the "lowest" position in a situation. But in fact, there are no real "high" or "low" positions in the world—there is only the right place for each individual at a given time and place, within the organic Whole. Some have rejected the idea of adopting humility as an attitude because they were erroneously trained in shame and self-deprecation in the name of humility. These people usually shift to a rebellious form of rigid pride and an inflated sense of self as a defense against the pain of this false understanding. I have seen other people choose permanent identification with the poor and struggling—"the people"—in the name of humility. Some of these folks feel righteous in their sense of separation from the rich and powerful, yet they may actually be practicing a greater form of arrogance than that of the people they presume are snobs! Humility is neither high nor low, rich nor poor. It is taking your rightful place *now,* and serving the good of the Whole from that place.

I remember hearing a friend of Martin Luther King Jr. describe the constant struggle Dr. King felt about being in his position in the civil rights movement. He often felt that he was inadequate for the job, that he lacked some of the skills and qualities that he perceived were necessary for this leadership. And yet this "place" was continually offered to him by the mysterious force of this powerful movement, and it was his place alone to take. How fortunate for our whole nation that he had the humility to continue to accept this position despite his nagging insecurity.

Every one of us is gifted in some regard. It seems that our life situations will consistently ask us to serve the good of the Whole with these gifts, which come out of our character and our nature. Our gifts contribute to the balance and health of human society. I know someone who has an uncanny knack for enhancing the physical comfort of any environment he is in for more than a day. He serves the comfort of those around him with apparent grace and ease; it comes out of who he is. I know someone else who has an intuitive radar for errors and missing details, and he has been an invaluable worker in his jobs in warehouses and mail order businesses, where these skills really count. There are people who are natural counselors, and their good listening skills and easy empathy will attract the upset or needy person at any party or bus stop! Sometimes we find ourselves asking "Why am I always the one who ...?" Well, because you are. So you're the one who volunteers to stay to clean up after the party is over? Good! Do it. Humility asks you to give what you have to give, within practical limits.

I have known some bright and talented people who kept their light under a bushel basket because they were afraid to shine. They doubted their motives, their right to take up space; they served a false notion of humility. Every time God offered them an opportunity to shine, they backed off or sabotaged their own efforts so they wouldn't have too big of an impact on anything.

If Life is asking you to shine, it is a form of arrogance to refuse it. It is also a lack of perspective. You are not the best or the worst thing that has ever come along, you are just uniquely you, and it's your turn under the sun to grow and blossom, spread your seeds, and die. What if the prairie flowers refused to bloom because they were afraid they wouldn't be the best thing on the prairie, or that no one would really appreciate their effort? Humility is taking one's rightful place in the Universe.

I was introduced to another definition of humility by my mentor, Dr. Edith Stauffer. She taught me that humility is an attitude of perceiving another's needs as *they* see them, and the desire to serve those needs, if practical. That'll keep you busy on your spiritual path for a while. Another's needs, as *that person* understands them. It is so much easier to think that we know what someone else needs; what their priorities should be. The people around us may be telling us very clearly what they need with words or behavior, but if we don't have an attitude of humility in place, we can miss it entirely. We're busy trying to help them with needs we think they *should* have, and we're getting all upset about how ungrateful they are for our efforts!

Sometimes the practice of humility takes the form of accepting criticism. I used to have a tendency to feel crushed or very defensive if there was a hint of criticism coming in my direction. Yet many of the real turning points in my development were triggered by facing some uncomfortable truth about myself that someone managed to get through to me. Benjamin Franklin once said "Your faults are your obstacles, so you should be grateful to others for pointing them out to you."

At this point you may be saying to yourself, "Come on, what are you trying to be, a *saint*?" Well, yes. I *do* want to be a saint. I have had the privilege of meeting a few souls in this world who have mastered being human—who are saintly—and I have watched them in action. It looks really good to me. I observe that these people are first and foremost themselves, their personalities fully open and exalted like a summer rose. I once took a heartfelt problem of mine to such a person, who was surrounded by hundreds of people at the time. But she acted as if there were no one else in the room. Nothing was more important to her in that moment but serving my need as I understood it. This moment of total loving attention was like a healing balm for me.

It was in the company of a few souls on Earth that I realized humility is a power as radiant as the sun or as strong as a thundering waterfall in its ability to transform others. Power is the unimpeded expression of Spirit through a particular form or personality. I must regard my own efforts at humility and power with the same tenderness I would a baby bird that is learning to fly. My relationship to a saint is like that of a baby bird to a grown bird. I will forgive my awkward flapping and falling down, and smile at the screeches I emit. I trust that one day I will fly in the clear sky of my liberated Spirit.

"We ask ourselves, who am I
to be brillliant, gorgeous, talented, fabulous?
Actually, who are you not to be?
You are a child of God."
- Marianne Williamson

Loss

Loss is an event that I keep thinking of as an exception to normal life, an aberration—except this must be wrong because it happens so often. I have had many losses: a child, a best friend, a dog, a family business. If this sort of thing isn't happening to me right now, it's happening to someone I know or someone on the news. No matter how much I say that I understand that life is impermanent and not under my control, I admit it is still a shock to me when this proves itself true.

Every time I face a loss and am living through a time of grief, I remember a few things. I remember that the Universe is simultaneously dispassionate and compassionate towards its members. It is dispassionate in that it is no respecter of persons: it does not *care* how much money you lost, or how embarrassing this scandal is, or how gross the accident was, or how young the children are when your husband contracts a terrible illness. This cool dispassion is the meaning within the esoteric bumper sticker slogan, "Shit happens."

On the other hand, the Presence within this Universe is at the same time completely compassionate towards us when we are suffering through anything, large or small. When I am reeling from sudden loss, I turn vulnerably towards that Presence, and I find myself in a warm pocket of peace and benevolence amid my grief. My heart opens in love and compassion for myself and others, and I soften into the richness of the present moment. Every need I have is met as fast as I can think of it. Friends and strangers alike become emissaries of this love. At these times I think, *Ah, I understand now. I will always remember this.* This is the experience expressed on another bumper sticker, "Grace happens."

Then comes the problem of integrating my loss into daily life. This is difficult to accomplish gracefully. After I have granted myself a certain amount of time to be emotional and get some support, I rally myself and march back into normal life with thoughts like, *Come on, get back on the ball, back in the saddle, back into production.* But it's hard to accept being with grief for as long as it actually takes to emerge from it. I become painfully aware that no one is paying me for all the hours I seem to need to stare into space after a loss, and how impatient with myself I am when I am not capable of being at the top of my game at work. I find myself resisting being soft and vulnerable to the Presence in the way that I was in the midst of the crisis. And there are times when I cannot bear to walk forward for very long with the awareness of my real helplessness.

Yesterday morning I looked out my window and found a hurt sparrow lying on its back out in the cold. I ran outside and scooped it gently into my hands. My intention was to move it to a quiet place away from my dog so it could die undisturbed—its neck was obviously broken. But as I carried it, the bird looked into my eyes with a peaceful curiosity, apparently unafraid. It was so alive! I didn't have the heart to put some-body who was *really* looking at me down onto the hard ground to die. So I brought him inside. Like a child would, I put him in a shoebox with flannel rags and got him some water with "rescue remedy," which I fed him with an eye-dropper.

The adult, dispassionate part of me observed my futile behavior with wry acceptance. I knew the bird was going to die. But somehow I had to do this anyway.

My young daughter immediately became absorbed in the process of "helping the bird." Even though I warned her we would try this only for a little while, and the bird would probably die, she became passionately bonded with "her" bird within moments. She fed him water punctually on the half hour, cooed encouragement, and brought him pictures to look at while he was resting. She kept seeing signs that the bird's condition was dramatically improving as a result of her faith and effort. I tried to reflect reality to her from time to time, but it was obvious that she wouldn't accept it.

The sparrow died that evening. My daughter was stunned and hurt to approach his shoebox and find him still, his bright eyes closed. She threw herself into my arms and cried hot tears while still shaking her head in disbelief. She had to tell me the exact details of her latest nursing efforts, and exactly how he looked when she found him dead. She gazed deeply into space, absorbed in sorrow as we rocked together in the dim room.

The next morning, she needed to take his body out and look at it. Again, the look of grave sorrow on her face. She shook her head a little and sighed, still not quite believing. She insisted that we take several photos of him before putting him back into his burial bag. Then we drew pictures for her to take to school—one of her feeding the living bird with a dropper, and one of her crying as she looked at him in death. She showed the pictures to her classmates and told them the story. That night I asked her how she felt about it and she said, "I'm still sad, but not as much. It's passing."

It seems to me that most of us are like children, bonding passionately to people and things with the cry of, "Mine!" Then we experience desolation when we discover that they aren't. At these times the Wise One within whispers, "I know this really hurts. This is just the way it is." We rock together in the dim light, pondering, staring into space. And healing comes.

"See! I will not forget you—I have carved you on the palm of my hand."
- Isaiah 49:15

THE GIFTS OF CATASTROPHE

Catastrophe ("a sudden and terrible disaster; a calamity") is a normal feature of life here on planet Earth. Catastrophe happens—it visits regularly on a personal and on a collective basis. Wars, murders, abductions, invasions, epidemics, tsunamis, violent accidents—it's been this way in every place and in every time. Peace and stability reign for a while in a family or a culture, yet even those eras are peppered and pocked by the presence of smaller catastrophes. Spills, collapses, the disfigurement of a black eye, a favorite toy broken—there is no escaping catastrophe because it is part of the curriculum in the school of Life. Besides the need to eat, breathe, love and be loved, the most common human need may be the need to treat one's own particular degree of post traumatic stress disorder! PTSD may be more normal than "normal."

Catastrophe is here to stay, and it cracks us wide open in the moment to bring to us the kind of goodness that only catastrophe can bring. And these days, most of us are aware that we dwell on the edges of the largest catastrophe in human history: the disruptive planetary transformation that will be coming down on us for decades to come due to the impact of global warming on the biosphere. As anxiety-producing as this situation is, I can't help but think good will come out of it because we will be challenged to the core of our collective being to learn how to live in harmony with the Earth, and how to live with the consciousness that we are one being: a fully awakened humanity.

I remember when a tornado hit South Minneapolis in the early 1980s. My friend and I were driving around to see the uprooted trees and crashed-in roofs. Many other people were walking or driving around, doing the same thing. As we drove slowly around a street corner with the window open, I met eyes with a man standing there. With childlike wonder his smile dawned wide, and he spoke his thought to me in a reverent voice: "It's a *catastrophe!*" He was unconsciously delighted with how shocking this was. And so were we. There's something oddly refreshing mixed with the horror of seeing something large that is utterly demolished. And we yearn to reach out to people who are caught in the bull's-eye of a catastrophe's hit. We want to help them, to serve them, to let them know that we care about what happened. Boundaries dissolve and universal love and selfless service flow into the space that catastrophe has brought into being.

I have experienced a number of catastrophes in my life. When I used to think like a victim I believed that I was dealt more than my fair share of dramatic personal events, but now I like to frame it in a positive way. Clarissa Pinkola Estes, author of *Women Who Run With the Wolves*, suggests that you should count up your scars and wear them proudly as a member of the "Scar Clan"—the more the better for those of us who have a big appetite for experience. So the litany for me looks like this: As a child my house burned down, my appendix ruptured, my family had an alcoholic crisis that nearly killed one of my parents, and I was assaulted when I was a teenager. As an adult I became seriously ill for about three months, my husband's business went bankrupt, he was injured, sick, and unemployed for two decades, I had three miscarriages (one of them life-threatening), our house was half destroyed by a flood, and someone close to me attempted suicide.

I suspect that each of us has a litany of personal catastrophes, and they are electrified points in a time line that is otherwise filled with "normal" life and lesser issues. I don't know how my list compares with other people's, or whether to name my life catastrophes as major or minor, in general terms. I have met a person who witnessed his father murdering his mother as a child. That's major. I know an active man who fell off a roof at work and became completely paralyzed from the neck down for the rest of his life. Major. For another person the catastrophe is a series of smaller losses packed into the same period of time: the divorce/job layoff/mother's stroke, all within six months of each other. Major? Minor? There is no way of judging that. When catastrophe visits us, it blows hurricane winds through the middle of our stable lives and tender hearts. But like the man looking at a tornado's destruction, those terrible experiences become our favorite stories to tell later, our dark treasures. The spectrum of catastrophic experiences unites every person to every other person on this Earth.

On September 11, 2001, Americans experienced a collective catastrophe as we watched the Twin Towers fall, and thousands of people die in moments before our eyes. We gazed in grief and horror upon that image for months afterwards: two flaming buildings and a wall of dust that signaled the end of an era for America. We lost our collective innocence that day, and the sense of invulnerability to attack that made us unique for a long time among the nations. We acted out our post traumatic stress disorder for years afterwards with attempts to control airline hijacking, kill nameless Muslim terrorists, and the doomed hunt for the chief-named villain, Osama Bin Laden. As someone said at that time, "Now we are all Israelis." Now we too as a people have shuddered together with the loss of life from a sudden attack, as have the Israelis, the people of Sarajevo, children in East Timor, wedding guests in Afghanistan, and peasants in Russia. As candles were lit and flowers piled up at the gates of American embassies around the world, we received the love and good will that flowed to us from anonymous citizens everywhere. So much goodness (disguised as patriotism) swelled out of American citizens in response to our catastrophe, but as I write this essay in 2008, I see that the good will of the world has ebbed away from us because once again we turned our craving for safety into war-making. I wish that every nation would resolve to respond to the shock and pain of terrorist attacks with an attitude of peace and forgiveness, and the steadfast refusal to create more of the same energy, as did the leaders of Bali when their nation faced the catastrophe of a terrorist attack upon ordinary citizens.

One of the classic outcries from people after an event of such magnitude is, "How could God let this happen to innocent people?!" In a way, this statement shows our innocence most clearly, because God never promised us protection from blind, amoral Nature. We are part of that Nature, and what happens to us here in

Nature is natural. We desperately invoke God's protection from pain and death and catastrophic loss, and yet God Herself has no problem with these things. On the contrary, what if catastrophe is part of God's Universal Creative Toolbox? In the Hindu tradition, God is seen as a trinity. There is God the Creator, God the Sustainer, and God the Destroyer. Brahma, Vishnu, and Shiva, also known as Kali. In this understanding, God spends time creating, sustaining, and destroying entire worlds and universes just for the fun of it. For Westerners, appreciation of the destructive aspect of God is perhaps an acquired taste. We are still attached to the notion that we are in control, and that we have dominion over the Earth with our sciences and our social order. And we don't. Even though we Christians carry an image of an authoritative God barking out laws and orders, and a gentle Christ helping the lion and the lamb lie down together, we are also in relationship with Kali, the Goddess of Destruction, whether we believe in her or not.

Kali dances wildly, wearing a necklace of skulls, and her fingernails drip blood. We are afraid of her, but we need her as surely as we need the pacific blessings of Christ. She renews the Earth with prairie fires and volcanoes, and she doesn't sweat a few thousand human bodies if that happens to come along with it. Kali knows that we are more than our limited bodies and personalities. We are the Self, eternally free from the limitations of birth and death, the particles of body, soul, and elements endlessly recycling and reassembling in God's play of consciousness. Kali has no guilt or regret as she whacks away with her sword in her whirling dance through the Universe. Good old Kali. She especially loves to destroy our ego and its illusions.

I've made friends with bloody Kali, and accepted her as one of my teachers during two catastrophes I've experienced. One happened to another person and one happened to me. On a hot summer night I was shaken out of sleep by the distressed cries of a man who had just been beaten up and knifed. Without thinking, I ran out to him barefoot and in my nightgown. A few others gathered, and we all helped in comforting him, getting medical help, and talking to the police. Later, as I sat and sipped tea in my kitchen in an attempt to calm down, I was aware of surges of ecstasy inside me. It wasn't just adrenalin. Something in me was singing with joy in the unity found in serving someone made vulnerable by catastrophe. I stared with odd fulfillment at the bloodstains on my dirty toes.

The other incident, my personal catastrophe, introduced me to Mother Kali in a moment that is seared into my psyche and is one of my most treasured scars. When I miscarried my baby at nearly five months, the onset of that loss was sudden and dramatic, awakening me from sleep at five a.m. with a gushing hemorrhage. From a sound sleep, I sprang from my bed and sprinted down the hall to the bathroom, shouting for my husband as I ran. I sat on the toilet, cupping a perfect little fetus in my hands, and stared at it in wonder and surprise while my blood fell all around me like a steady rain. My mouth was wide open and so was his. It was a tragicomic moment—I felt like the baby and I were looking at each other and saying, "Huh??!!" That little open mouth reminded me of all the human "huh's?!" that ever were.

Though my heart was pounding with fear and surprise, there was a calm wonder and sweetness welling up within me at the same time. The room seemed very bright and clear and special. My husband and I looked at the fetus and each other, and when we both realized that all three of us had our mouths agape in the same way, something broke open between us and we actually *laughed* into each others eyes. It was a moment of a great transcendent love between us. In that moment, it seemed like the bathroom walls dissolved like a thin veil to reveal a Universe surrounding me, a Universe filled with creation and destruction played out on an unshakable foundation of unutterable love. I bowed a little bow to Kali's presence in the room—I could just about hear her ankle bracelets jingling as she danced. Then we proceeded with the rest of the drama: shock, ambulance, hospital, home care, community support, grief, hospital bills, getting up again. But I will always remember that sparkling moment of catastrophe in the bathroom.

The Hindus say that we live in the age of

Kali, and I can believe it—or why would so many of our blockbuster movie hits be concerned with disaster of one kind or another? We *liked* seeing the gorgeous, invincible *Titanic* succumb to the vagaries of human error and the icy cold waves of the North Atlantic! And every night, of our own free will, millions of viewers settle down in their pajamas to hear the stories and view the images of violence, loss, struggle, and shocking events that our mass media pump right into our soft living rooms for our consumption. There is nothing that makes a better news day than catastrophe, and the news makers roam far away to find catastrophes if there are no local ones to report. The reporters doggedly run to the "ground zero" point of the most pain to be found, and pursue the people whose hearts are visibly breaking, or the ones whose hearts are wide open to their self-less heroism. The camera seeks them, finds them, rivets our attention upon the very heart of that pain, and that selfless love. We watch, unable to tear ourselves away from the screen, in deep meditation on those images. Why? Because God is there. God is there.

The things planned before the world began
come upon us suddenly,
so that in our blindness we say
that they are chance.
But God knows better.
Constantly and lovingly
He brings all that happens to its best end.
When a soul holds on to God in trust—
this is the highest worship it can bring.
- Julian of Norwich

Getting Up Again

"All the world's a stage,
and all the men and women merely players."
- William Shakespeare

There are times in your life when you feel like an actor in a play that has suddenly been rewritten without warning. There you are, performing your role as you have studied and rehearsed it, and suddenly there is a flurry of stagehands removing the familiar props, and your leading partner is cut from the scene. You stare into dim spaces outside the footlights seeking the face of the director, and feebly call, "Line?" Death, injury, divorce, disease, business failure ... who doesn't know the feeling of having the rug pulled out from under you and hitting the hard ground of reality with a sickening thud? We all go through these things at times, and we face the difficult task of getting up again.

The phoenix is an ancient symbol of rebirth, a triumph of the spirit's renewal after apparent destruction. Originating in Egyptian mythology, the phoenix is a bird that periodically consumes itself by fire and rises renewed from its own ashes. It would be nice if people could rise immediately from their wreckage with a flurry of wings and golden sparks flying, but the process is usually more gritty and pedestrian than that. It looks like hobbling to your knees, pulling yourself up with some outside support, and leaning on something while you attempt to breathe evenly. Then you limp slowly forward on a dimly-lit trail, the horizon obscured by undergrowth. Eventually your strength returns and your trail meets up with a larger track and a clear view. Until then, you have to proceed with an ample supply of support, perspective, hope, and will.

When you are suffering from a personal loss or catastrophe, it helps to get some support from others who really understand your situation. You are not alone. There are others who are going through something similar right now, and they may have a larger compassion and bigger ears for the details of your sorrow than your friends who are tired of hearing about it. These days, there are support groups for just about everything you can think of.

There are also experts who can offer some experienced perspective on your recovery process. It helps to hear that you are dealing with something that many others have faced; that it was not a personal attack on you for some imagined unworthiness. We need to be reminded that healing takes time. I have heard that it takes at least three years to grieve and integrate the divorce of a long marriage. When my friend fell off a roof and suddenly became paralyzed from the neck down, a rehabilitation therapist told him that it takes an average of five years to come to acceptance and happiness after such a change.

I think that hope is not a *feeling,* it is a *discipline.* Hope is a set of behaviors and attitudes you adopt to carry you forward as if your life matters, even though at the moment you may feel that it doesn't. When you are facing a time of heavy emotion and lack of direction, it is an act of hope to tend to health habits like eating and sleeping, and to keep a minimum level of beauty and order in your appearance and environment. When sailors are kept ashore by stormy seas, they mend nets and clean the boat for future sailing because they know that the storm is finite and work at sea will call them again.

It is natural to experience depression after a major loss. It is the discipline of hope that prevents the chemistry of depression from getting too great a hold on you and setting in for a long time. Vitamins, exercise, fresh air, and sunlight will help your body continue to clear through this stress. Listening to music, especially stringed instruments, is a balm for a sore heart and jangled nerves. A good hearty cry in someone's arms is certainly called for too. You can discipline yourself to stop negative self-talk in your mind and switch your thoughts to positive statements. And though you may feel lacking in spiritual inspiration at the moment, you can build your physical strength and will until vision is kindled in your life again.

Your will is the spiritual mechanism by which goals are attained and new dreams become manifested. If you are experiencing a lack of dreams or goals, you can still go about the business of strengthening and toning your will until it has a new job to do. Establishing a routine and sticking to it is one way of strengthening your will. Rhythmic exercise, drumming music, and accomplishing small distasteful tasks will also help. I strengthen my will by insisting that I be punctual for appointments—I am usually ten minutes late. The mere accomplishment of being on time for a few days in a row begins to make me feel strong and toned, ready for larger challenges.

Strengthening the will is done by the same principles as strengthening muscles on an exercise machine: Isolate and focus on a number of small individual tasks in your life, and work at each of them regularly. It may seem silly or futile some days, but strength of will builds, and eventually a zest for a new challenge does too. And when that zest is there, it attracts inspiration for new roles and goals in your life. At this point you can usually look back at your earlier catastrophe and feel some appreciation for its occurrence, and sometimes even see how it was necessary for you to let go of that precious something that was wrestled out of your hands.

I never used to comprehend why anyone

would want to watch football on TV. It seemed so brutal to me. But I think now that some of the charm of this sport is watching someone get up again after getting sacked! After one of my losses I watched some football and was enlivened by the sight of these huge guys jumping up again after apparently being creamed by a mighty tackle. They emerge from under this pile of equally huge guys, shake their heads a little, bounce up and down a couple of times, and jog back to the line with a little spank of support from a nearby buddy. They don't take it personally, because this is all part of the game.

History provides us with numerous examples of people getting up after having the wind knocked out of them. Wars and earthquakes have shivered through the human race time after time, leaving wounds and wreckage in their wake. And yet cities get rebuilt, and people fall in love again. Poets sing the stories of the heroes, and the mother cries her impassioned, "Why?" to caring witnesses. The experience of loss and getting up again is an integral part of the human adventure.

I learned something special about a spaceship that was sent up some years ago as an ambassador to unknown civilizations outside our solar system. Among the artifacts of human culture is a piece of music chosen to represent the human spirit. Out of ten thousand songs that were proposed, the song that speeds towards our unknown friends in the Universe is a Bulgarian folk song that embodies a message of mourning, strength, determination, and the thirst for freedom. It is wonderful that our scientists chose to be vulnerable to the unknown witnesses in the Universe to say, "Hi! We're here. It isn't easy. But we keep getting up again. Freedom calls."

After the final no there comes a yes
and on that yes the future of the world depends.
- Wallace Stevens

THE EXPERIENCE OF FORGIVENESS

*Forgiveness: The profound experience
of releasing an expectation
that has been causing one to suffer*

*Unconditional Love: A refreshing Universal energy
that restores us to wholeness*

The experience of forgiveness is profound
and refreshing! Forgiveness changes us physically
and emotionally, dissolving the stagnant weight
of resentment and flooding our bodies with
fresh new energy. It mends our tattered personal
boundaries, and empowers us to move forward
with more hope and creativity in operation than
when we were holding our grudges. When we
do the thorough and gritty work that goes into
releasing trauma from the past, we reestablish our
connection with our spiritual Source, and that
Source rewards us with a palpable sense of light
and lightness. We find ourselves on new ground.

I think it's safe to say that there aren't

too many people who actually *want* to forgive someone who's really hurt them, but we do want to feel better. It's kind of like having a toothache and recognizing the need for dental work. You don't *want* to go to the dentist and feel more pain for an hour, so you stay in denial for a while. But the pain persists, and you know that you'll feel better if you do something about it. So you muster the discipline to make the appointment, go through the experience, and get the job done. In the same way, we often put off naming the fact that we need to forgive someone, because then we have to *do* it!

Maybe we know we want to forgive someone, but it seems hard and we don't know how. Maybe we are afraid that if we forgive someone who has hurt us, we will make ourselves too vulnerable and set ourselves up for further hurt. Perhaps we can't forgive because we feel that what was done is unjust, and we think forgiveness implies that we condone injustice. (It doesn't.) Or it could be that we find so much satisfaction in feeling *right* in judging another, and we'd rather be right than be at peace. Usually, people are ready to forgive when they tire of the struggle and the story playing over and over in their heads. The need for peace finally outweighs the need to be right.

I once taught a short class which began with a woman defiantly raising her hand and declaring, "I just want you to know at the outset that I don't think it's even remotely possible to forgive my fiancé and my best friend for having an affair three weeks before our wedding." She received nods of support from the other class members as she explained that she'd already broken ties with both of them, but she felt like a basket case and didn't know how to go on. She didn't want to forgive them, but she couldn't eat, sleep, or function at work, and she didn't know what else to do. I encouraged her to go along with the exercises in the workshop that she was willing to, and we then heartily engaged the whys and wherefores of forgiveness for a few hours.

After we had all practiced getting in touch with our Higher Power through a number of simple exercises, she raised her hand again and said, "I want you to know that I think there is a *tiny shred of possibility* that I can forgive them and move on." "Good!" I congratulated her. "All you need is a tiny shred of faith and a tiny bit of willingness. Then when you do the steps of FORGIVENESS, you will find the healing you're looking for." And because she had already cried and raged her fill, and was so ready to feel better, she forgave both of them and herself completely in a total of two hours' private work, and found permanent relief from this hurt.

Permanent relief? I hear you say. Can we really get permanent healing from the pain of our biggest wounds? We can. Forgiveness is a natural and a transformational process—like fire that burns wood to ashes. If you burn a log to ash, you don't wake up the next day and find a whole log again. It's been changed. In the same way, if you work through an injury in all the ways that your whole being requires, as in THE EIGHT STEPS OF FORGIVENESS—you are changed. Your own body tells you that this is true. I once forgave my husband's business for stressing us out for years and then going belly up anyway. As I completed the last step of forgiveness, I literally felt something go *"sproing!"* and pop out of my chest, leaving my heart feeling light and free. I didn't know that I was carrying my pain about that business as a burden on my heart until I felt it leave me.

Sometimes we hold on to our resentment towards someone whom we love because we feel that the resentment is the only bond we have with them. A woman at one of my workshops hesitated just as she was about to forgive her dad for being incestuous with her as a child. Even though after seven years of therapy there was nothing more to say or do with the horror of it, she just couldn't let it go. She thought she would feel like an orphan with no father at all if she forgave him and stopped holding her grudge against him—it was her bond with him. I encouraged her to turn her heart towards her Higher Power as a Father, and let her fallible earthly dad off the hook at last. When she did this and completely released all of her expectations of her dad, she became flooded with buried memories of a good connection with him. She found her peace. In addition to healing her relationship with her dad, this woman reported to me later, "It's like all my senses woke up that day. I was numb before. Now I smell flowers, and hear birds, and feel the breezes as I do my work as a postal carrier. I came alive again that day."

This works for forgiving moms, too—if we turn to God the Mother and release all our disappointed expectations of our human mothers, we find a Divine Source pouring in the nurturing we crave. Nobody has to remain an orphan in this world!

From time to time I am blessed to witness that people can forgive the unforgivable. Once I taught an UNCONDITIONAL LOVE AND FORGIVENESS workshop at a retreat center in central Wisconsin. On the first evening, a woman I'll call Liz shyly revealed that she sought healing from the trauma of having been raped by her minister a number of years earlier. Her face was strained and gray, and her posture was tight and protected—the personal hell that she lived in was visible to all of us. The compassion in the room from the other sixty participants was full and warm as she spoke, and I knew that I was meant to work with her that weekend.

Over the course of the next two days, I watched Liz gathering her will—the first step towards forgiveness—and seek in prayer and community to find the strength to completely forgive this man for his terrible act. She wanted to free herself of any further entanglement with him or with that moment. On the last day of the workshop I helped her descend fully into the hate and poison left within her from this experience, and in the course of an hour she forgave her rapist completely, step by step. Sixty people sat patiently through her foul language and her vivid imaginary castration of her assailant. Releasing your emotional truth is the second step of forgiveness. As we moved on through the third and fourth steps I found myself wondering *Will this really work? Can even this be forgiven?* Her powerful work pushed on the edges of my own capacity to forgive and my own faith in the process. However, we both persisted and—faithful as the sun—the light of forgiveness dawned.

As Liz reached the final two steps of forgiving, and reached toward her Spiritual

Source for healing, the hair on my arms and head was standing up because the room was electric with Spirit's powerful restorative energies. It was clear to me that her nervous system was being flushed clean of the habitual patterns installed when she was victimized. Liz emerged from her hour-long journey looking as pink and open as a full-blown summer rose. There was a remarkable beauty and healthy vulnerability in her face and body, and she declared with certainty that the trauma was "all gone!" Everything was silent for a few moments except for the soft weeping of a few of the witnesses, and then there was such an outburst of whooping and hugging and talking! I think sixty other people simultaneously decided that they too had the courage to get to work forgiving people on their lists. If she could do *that* ....

If that wasn't enough to blow my mind, Liz told me later how it was that she came to be in my workshop at all. She was traveling across the country from Idaho to Massachusetts in her car, and at the eastern edge of Wisconsin she followed an impulse to stop in a church to pray.

She prayed again to be healed of her hurt. As she left the church, a stray flyer on a pew caught her attention. It was an advertisement for my workshop. An inner voice told her, "Go there!" *So, she backtracked two hundred miles to arrive at my workshop just as it was starting, and got what she needed.* When I heard this, it assured me once again that the Universe itself is conspiring to help us find wholeness, and forgiveness is a gift we all deserve to enjoy.

"For 'tis sweet to stammer one letter
of the Eternal's language;
on Earth it is Forgiveness!"
- Henry Wadsworth Longfellow

The Eight Steps of Forgiving Another Person

1. **Use your will**. Decide to move forward into a new attitude and greater freedom.

2. **Express your emotional truth.** Speak honestly. Vent to your satisfaction. Entertain a few revenge fantasies if necessary.

3. **Cancel the expectations you are holding in your mind.** Break them down into parts, shift them into preferences, dissolve each one completely.

4. **Reach out to the resources of the Universe to get what you need in this situation.**

5. **Reestablish your boundaries:** give the other person responsibility for their actions, and visualize your strong personal space.

6. **Reach to your Spiritual Source for healing**. Draw healing light down into your body, mind, and emotions through your crown chakra. (The top of your head.)

7. **Send light and love to the other person,** or to their Higher Power, just as they are.

8. **See the good in them** or in the spiritual lesson of the situation.

LIVING YOUR PURPOSE

"I am on a spiritual journey. I am seeking my purpose." So many times in recent years I have enjoyed the sparkle in the eye of someone who has discovered a hearty appetite for personal truth and living purposefully. There is a vitality to these people, a focused yearning, and a desire for insight and fulfillment that brings the very air around them to life. Sometimes there is also a sense of anxiety present, a feeling of having wasted time previous to this, the gnawing fear that time is passing quickly and will run out before this purpose is discovered and fulfilled. I feel the urge to pat them soothingly and say, "Relax. It's OK. Don't make everything such a big deal—you're doing fine."

On the other hand, I know people who are so relaxed and self-satisfied that they are, in effect, almost asleep. They have cut their little grooves with their habits and their schedules, they have perfectly adapted themselves to the bumps and fissures in their relationships, and they do not stray much from the predictable patterns that have been established in their peer group or in their own conditioned minds. They live like pleasant zombies, and it's hard to tell some days if anyone is home. My hand twitches because I want to grab them by the elbow, shake it, and say, "Who are you?! Why don't you find out? What are you waiting for?"

Why does this bother me? Why do I notice it so much when someone is in a taut or a loose posture in relation to the issue of purpose? Maybe because they mirror for me my own faulty state of tension in relation to living my purpose. Faulty? Could there be a right and a wrong about this? Not really. This is more a matter of aesthetic appreciation: One can live one's life like a well-strung violin in the hands of a master, or a slack and dusty old fiddle lying in your grandfather's attic. Each of these has its points of interest, but I prefer the first way—the way of self-mastery. Because, simply put, a human being who is fully living his or her purpose with relaxation and focus is a beautiful thing to see.

Spiritual maturity is a state of being that can embrace the paradox in life. For each and every truth you discern, there is an equal and opposite truth that is operative in another situation or in the same situation at another time. And there is a great Truth contained and balanced between all of the lesser truths you can think of, a Truth that is not told in words. A mature mind that expresses itself peacefully from the center of this Truth, while maintaining a full awareness of paradox, is as precious as a full-blown rose, blessing its surroundings with its pure essence. This intrinsic beauty is the "why" behind seeking one's purpose.

"Seeking purpose" is a paradoxical activity. It is both necessary and unnecessary to seek it. The key to discovering and fulfilling one's purpose is to just relax and love what you have—no, it's to get going and create what you truly want—no, it's to relax sometimes and get going at other times—no, it's to do them both at the same time in different areas of your life—and as the saying goes, "Nothing that you do really matters, but it's very important that you do it anyway." You see the challenge here? There are paradoxical truths about seeking one's purpose that we need to understand and live by if we want our souls to sing well in the chorus of human expression.

So, you don't know what your purpose in this life is? *Relax!* You haven't missed the boat. Your purpose cannot leave without you. You have time. In fact, unless you are passed out under the bed with a bottle of vodka in your hands, there is a 95% chance that you are fulfilling your purpose just beautifully. (Even if you are hiding under the bed, who knows what God-like role you play for the dust mites?!) Maybe you just haven't noticed yet what it is you are doing here. Give up your anxiety and relax into the effortless flow of expression that is simply *you*. Accept the true limits of your particular personality and don't try to be anyone else. Between the moment of your first breath and the moment of your death, there is plenty of time for you to fulfill your purpose.

You don't know what your purpose in this life is? What are you waiting for? *Get going!* Today is a good day to start. Time is passing quickly. There are ways of being yourself that you desire but haven't dared to try yet. Don't waste this precious opportunity to be alive and experience things that you want. There's nothing stopping you but false limitations. You can use your will and your Higher Wisdom to discover and fulfill your purpose. Our world desperately needs your gifts and service, freely given. Don't hold back!

In fact, both of these directives, *Relax* and *Get Going*, are correct in different ways, for there are a number of levels to the subject of purpose. Everything and everyone, from a mossy rock to a human being, is fulfilling at least one level of purpose, due to the mere fact of their existence. I call this level **existential purpose**. You exist because you exist. You can add a few skills onto that and leave society in a little better condition than when you arrived, and you have a **social purpose.** This is about what job you have or what career or vocation you pursue. You can engage with life as a classroom of learning, loving, and service, and you have a **spiritual purpose**. You can pair up with other people and share your complementary skills, and you've got purpose in partnership, or **symbiotic purpose**. Therefore, you can choose to call on more of your unused brain capacity and advance the whole thing farther along. Yes! The human being alone has the power of influencing the evolution of our species. You can consciously serve the collective *evolutionary purpose*.

The relaxing thing about looking at purpose in this way is that you can do any amount of it that you choose. You can have a wonderful career, be a fairly decent person, and touch some lives in a pleasant way, and never once ponder a greater meaning than that. You can hang out and take the path of least resistance, and be someone's loyal son. You can embrace the new technologies of body/mind transformation and take yourself higher and higher into the clear mountain air of higher consciousness, despite the fact that you have a mundane job at the post office. You can be born with Downs Syndrome, live on government aid, and warm the hearts of people around you with your innocent and loving disposition. On this level, we are all doing just fine.

And yet, there is something about the nature of the human being that insists on asking,

Why? and clamoring for more. There is something creative hard-wired into our genes that bides its time and eventually explodes outward in a surprising moment of genesis that initiates a period of divine restlessness and growth. Who knows what or who governs these cycles of rest and creativity? It's a mystery. I invite you to explore this mystery. Relax, and get going!

The Lord is inside you, and also inside me;
you know the sprout is hidden inside the seed ...
Look around inside.
The blue sky opens out farther and farther,
the daily sense of failure goes away,
the damage I have done to myself fades,
a million suns come forward with light,
when I sit firmly in that world.
- Kabir

Our Common Human Purpose

Anyone and everyone can live purposefully if they want to. It doesn't matter if you are very young or very old, schooled or unschooled, pretty or plain. It doesn't matter what your IQ is, and you don't need start-up capital to get on with it. It doesn't even matter what kind of a mess you've made of your life until now. You can embrace this purpose today, and immediately begin to reap the reward of knowing you are living a worthy life. What is this purpose—our common human purpose? *I am here to learn and to love.* I learned this from my Aunt Ann.

My Aunt Ann was a committed alcoholic all her life. You could count on her to be drunk most of the time. She tried a few AA meetings once, but it never "took." She was well-adjusted to her character defects, and much more interested in satisfying her curiosity about life and other people than doing any serious personal housecleaning. So, drunk she remained.

Nevertheless, Aunt Ann never lacked company for long. She was warm, witty, and insightful, and despite the fact that she slurred her words, she was a great conversationalist.

Aunt Ann lived in a high-rise on the North Side of Chicago, and received regular visits from her son John, his wife Meg, and their children Brigid and George. She needed a little looking after because she had drunk away the use of her legs, and used a wheelchair. John and Meg scolded my aunt in fear and exasperation when they came and found her passed out on the bathroom floor in a puddle. She frequently sported lumps and bruises, and once even a sprained arm, but nothing phased her.

"God, Mom! I told you to use those hand-rails we put in. How long have you been on the floor?"

"Oh, Jeez, Johnny—I don't know. Did you bring my whiskey? How's Brigid? Is she feeling better this week?"

My sister Hannah encouraged me to visit Aunt Ann when I came to town. Hannah, a writer, enjoyed plying Aunt Ann with questions about our family life in the 1920s and 30s. Despite the astonishing amount of alcohol her brain cells were swimming in, Aunt Ann's memory and her present-time faculties were incredibly clear. Young Hannah always left from her visits feeling invigorated and nourished by stories.

"Go see her, Mare," said Hannah. "She's so much fun and she's as sharp as a tack."

I did. I waited patiently in the hall for Aunt Ann to unlock her door. I could hear her fumbling with the locks and swearing under her breath for several minutes. When the door finally swung open and I looked down at my tiny aunt in her tiny wheelchair, I could see it must have been hard for her to get the top chain off the door. It was high over her head.

"Well, Mary Brigid!" she exclaimed in that familiar gravelly voice. "It's so *good* to see you! Come in, come in …."

My aunt tip-tip-toed her wheelchair steadily down her linoleum hallway ahead of me, her little feet covered in those absurd hospital slippers with the pom-poms. Her head was held high and her thick shock of uncombed white hair radiated independent self-expression. Her cigarette smoke streamed delicately behind her like a banner in a parade. I felt like a visiting dignitary.

"Your mother tells me you married a great guy—Frank? Fred! And you've opened a business together. What do you sell?" She leaned forward, ready for all the news.

I gave Aunt Ann the full report. Her bright blue eyes absorbed every word with rapt attention, and her smoke ascended thoughtfully to the ceiling. As I talked, she asked me a lot of questions, and occasionally declared, "Well, isn't that wonderful?!" I felt so good. The sunlight poured like a blessing through her high-rise windows. The half-empty bottle of whiskey on the table glowed like liquid amber. The scattered newspaper on the sofa could only hold good news ... what was this feeling? My heart was warm and my person was safe as I talked with this old blue-veined sprite of an aunt. *What is this? Oh, yes. This is what Love feels like.*

One day Aunt Ann's son Ralph came to officiate at one of our cousin's weddings. Ralph was a Catholic priest, and was enduring a long-term dilemma about whether to remain in the Church. He did a nice job anyway, as he always does, and later at the reception he found himself sitting with a thoughtful Aunt Ann.

"Ralph—" she said slowly, "What is the purpose of life?" Ralph didn't know until that moment that he knew the answer.

"Mom—the purpose of life is to learn and to love."

"To learn and to love … yes … that must be it … I like that … Thanks, son." "Sure, Mom."

The next Tuesday, Aunt Ann's daughter-in-law Meg went to Aunt Ann's home for her regular visit. They always watched her soap opera together at noon. Meg was surprised to find the door unlocked. She was even more surprised to find Aunt Ann sleeping peacefully on the couch, neatly tucked under an afghan with her hands folded. She was wearing a fresh house dress and for once her hair was combed. The sun streamed in on her old face as the television chattered softly in the background. "Mom?" said Meg, softly touching her knee.

There was no answer. Aunt Ann was dead. She had died of natural causes about fifteen minutes before Meg's predictable Tuesday visit. She somehow had the foresight to arrange to go with some dignity. At her funeral, we traded our favorite Aunt Ann stories, including the one about her last conversation with Ralph. We all came to the same conclusion that she apparently did—our Aunt Ann had learned and loved, and her life and her death were blessed with purpose.

"The purpose of life is to learn and to love."
- Cousin Ralph

THE BIG BECAUSE

"*Why?* I need to know why I have been spared so many times, while people who were leading better lives than I were not allowed to live?"

George's old face was troubled, and he struggled to keep his lip from trembling. As he talked, I could see memories passing through the screen of his mind like bad movies you wish you could forget. His fresh-faced buddies blown to bits in the nearby fox-hole ... the car accident that killed a young mother while he only got a scratch ... his friends and colleagues succumbing to strokes and cancer .... All of these people were charged with potential for success and a will to live, but they left their lives in mid-sentence. Meanwhile George himself struggled along, fighting chronic depression and inborn feelings of inadequacy. He straggled listlessly through a long, patchy career in which the only consistent note was mediocrity. The worst thing George endured was the haunting and accurate perception that even on his good days, his personality was a burden on the people he loved the most.

"*Why? Why does God want me to live when I'm just not good at it?*"

I suppose I could have responded, "For God's sake, man, you're just depressed! You need meds, now!" But the wiser part of me saw that this was deeper than garden-variety depression. I saw that he was really asking God this question, from his soul. He needed an answer—a fundamental truth to take in as medicine for this long-term guilt and malaise. And he was ready to hear the answer, so I knew that together we would find it. For some reason that probably has to do with my purpose, people have been discussing the meaning of life with me since I was young. Eventually I cultivated an intuitive process that allows me to seek and find guidance from Spirit for others for the times when they are unable to find it on their own. I did this now, with George.

Breathe ... notice my body tension ... breathe it away ... notice my thoughts and opinions, my desire to "fix" his pain ... breathe that away ... empty myself ... let go of outcome ... fill myself with a desire to serve the Highest Good

... pray sincerely to be of pure and loving service to this person, a worthy child of God ... still my mind ... quiet ... quieter ... like a lake with no ripples .... Now I ask a single question into that stillness: *"Why have You allowed George to live so long when it's been so hard?"*

The answer came immediately, in a loud and firm inner Voice: *"Because!"*

"Because?" I questioned meekly. I had never known God to be rude before.

"Yes, because. Absolutely."

The answer poured forth from within me in a rush of comprehension that I shared aloud with George.

"Because. Because I said so, George. Sometimes you just have to live a life because you're here, that's all. A human life is like a day—so fleeting in time. There are good days and bad days, productive days, sick days, quiet days, hectic days— they all pass on their way. George, you're just having a bad day. It's passing. There will be another day. Your loved ones know this in their hearts and are willing to tolerate you while you're having a bad day. Basically George, you just have to get through

it, that's all. That's all I'm asking of you. Don't waste any more time worrying about it. Just get through it. It'll be over soon and then there will be a new day."

I opened my eyes and peeked at George. His face hung slack, very relaxed. He opened his eyes, which now looked tired and peaceful.

"Thank you," he said thickly. "That was very helpful. If all I really have to do in this life is get through it, I'm very willing to do that. I'm glad that God understands that I'm just having a bad day. It's much better than believing I'm a bad person."

After George left, I mused on this for a while. *Because?* I always thought that each and every human life should be imbued with excellence and meaning, and something is going seriously wrong all the time because a lot of lives aren't so noble. And yet apparently God isn't bothered about this at all .... Because?

A KEY EXPERIENCE

"Oh, I hate this!" I cried in exasperation, as I slogged through the icy puddle looking for my keys.

"Come on, Mom—let's go home now. I'm cold!" My daughter stood with her shoulders hunched against the wet March winds.

"But that is my full set of keys with my favorite key-ring that your daddy gave me for Christmas!" I wailed, as I toed aside another chunk of floating ice to peer into the dark sodden grasses.

I straightened up and looked in despair at the sea of mud and melting snow that spread far and wide around me. Half an hour ago it seemed wild and daring to prance and splash with my daughter and my dog among the great old trees of our inner-city park. Now that my keys lay hidden somewhere in this muck, it seemed like the height of foolishness. The light was failing, so we walked dejectedly home. I imagined my car looking quiz-zically at me as we passed by and left it there by the curb instead of getting in and driving away.

My keys! I missed their weight in my pocket, and I thought of the lovely pewter keyring as my personal logo. It was a charming little open hand with a heart in its palm; it gave me a peaceful greeting every time I unlocked my door. It was well-crafted and expensive, as far as keyrings go. It would be embarrassing to ask Fred to buy me another one, especially since this was the third set of keys I had lost in recent memory. This time, I suspected that my husband would reach the end of his rope with this unfortunate habit of mine, his sense of security undermined by the fact that loose sets of our keys were at large in the inner city where we live. As I walked home with Tara and my disgracefully dirty dog, I had one foot firmly in shame, and the other foot in the awareness of an absolutely stunning red sunset ....

"Where were you running?" Fred asked.

It was the next day, and the park looked like a different world from yesterday's wet spring evening. The light glinted broad and bright on the hard surface of choppy ice that covered the huge lawn under the trees. The temperature had dropped overnight and winter's unyielding face had returned. My little keys could be encased anywhere in this opaque mess.

"From there ... to there ... to way over there ... and up there. It's pretty hopeless, really. I'm just going to report the loss at the park building in case they show up later in the spring."

"I'm going to keep looking," said Fred. "If children find them they're likely to keep the key ring anyway because it's so cute."

I left him there and trudged to the park building, resigned to the loss. I searched for the day coordinator, dodging basketballs and shouting to be heard above the throb of rap music and loud voices of a small group of teens. It was the middle of the school day, but there are always a lot of kids at loose ends in my neighborhood, looking for a place to be that is not school or their often unstable family situation. The community center constantly creates little programs to catch and serve the young lives that are flying about in chaos. I love the familiar whirl of vital energy here.

I found the coordinator, a friendly besieged man with a thumb-sucking eight-year old girl attached to his shirttails. He was moving what looked like a million folding chairs on a long cart from one place to another. The little girl trailed silently along with him on his duties. I didn't know him but I knew him: I had seen coordinators change here about every eighteen months for the last decade. Joe, Lenny, Sarah, Pat .... What's this guy's name? John. They all seem to have an incredible center of gravity amid this mayhem, and that famous Positive Attitude. I guess the turnover is so great because they are serving in society's front lines in the War Against Complete Disintegration. I couldn't help the love that poured out of my eyes as I told him I'd lost my keys in the park.

"Lost yer keys? Well I've got some fellows that don't got nothin' to do—they'll help you find yer keys!"

"Uh, no, that's OK. I could have lost them anywhere. If you could just take my number—"

"Pepe! Daniel! Mario! Come here, boys! We've got a job that needs doing! This lady's lost her keys."

"No, really, I don't think that we'll find

them while the ice is frozen—"

"These guys are great lookers," he said, "If anyone can find your keys, I bet they can! I'll offer an award of $1.00 to whoever sees them first!" His voice boomed with the Positive Attitude, but his eyes said, "*Lady, please! Help me out here.*"

I looked at the kids. They were all about nine. One of them was kicking the wall and making martial arts throws at the air. The other one had a wispy presence, and an unfocused stare that told me he wasn't quite convinced of his own existence. "Great lookers indeed," I thought. The third child stood at earnest attention, staring up at me with liquid brown eyes as he waited for my answer. The combined intelligence of his face and the insecurity of his posture pushed me over the edge and I signed up for The Key Project instead of going home like I had planned.

"Great, guys!" I said positively. "I really appreciate it. Let's go."

We walked out towards the great frozen lawn. Fred was methodically combing the distant perimeter of the park. He waved at us and continued his search. The raw wind flowed against us like ice water, and the boys were chattering with cold by the time we arrived at the huge general vicinity of my keys. None of them wore a jacket.

"Man, it's f—ing cold!" said Pepe.

"Where's your jacket, Pepe?" I asked. "Is it at the park building?"

"Yeah—I mean, no .... I don't know! Maybe I didn't wear one!" He attacked a tree with an awesome kung fu maneuver. Daniel stood vacantly nearby with his nose running. Mario clasped himself with his thin arms and said softly, "What do your keys look like?"

I described my keys to them. Pepe looked at me shrewdly. "Lady, is that little hand made out of real silver?" I told him that I thought it was pewter.

"Man, if that was real silver, I'd just keep them if I found them, and get some money for them."

He whirled off like a little dust devil out of season, looking here and there. Mario kept pace with me, looking carefully, his eyebrows making a line of concentration. Daniel continued to stand among the trees like a statue.

"I sure hope we find them," I said to Mario. "It had all of my important keys on it, and the key ring was a special gift from my husband."

"How much did that key ring cost, lady?" said a voice behind me. I was startled to find Pepe so close again. I told him about fifteen dollars.

"Then your husband should give us fifteen dollars if we find it instead of one dollar like the guy at the park."

I checked my irritation, remembering that I was now the director of the Key Project, and responsible for my words and actions.

"Well you know, Pepe, that kind of hurts my feelings when you say that."

Mario looked at me curiously, and Pepe paused in mid-whirl to ask, "Why? That's what it cost!"

"Sure," I said. "But I thought you were here to help me, not steal from me or expect a high fee. I'm upset about losing my keys—I need them. If you were upset about losing something special, I wouldn't take it from you if I found it.

If I said I was going to help you, I really would."

"I'll look over here ...." Pepe gave Daniel a little shove as he ran off.

Mario and I continued our methodical side-by-side search until it was too cold for me, even in my warm jacket. We called in the troops. Between the five of us, if you count Daniel, we had searched every inch of the expansive lawn.

"Thank you, boys. We gave it a good try."

"Maybe we need to dig under the ice," said Pepe, kicking into the ground with his sneaker. He was finally making eye contact with me and trying to be helpful.

"I think we looked pretty thoroughly. I guess I'll just have to get along without them.

"Mario"—I shook his hand, and he looked back at me shyly.

"Pepe"—he slapped at my hand and resumed his attack on the enemies in the wind.

"Dan"—he was already gone, slouching silently back towards the park building.

"It was nice to meet you, Mario. Thanks for looking so carefully."

He nodded shyly, and turned to go. My

keys were on the ground in front of his feet. Impossibly, the shiny little hand greeted him with its open heart.

"I found them!" he cried joyfully, pouncing on them and waving them over his head.

"MARIO!! MARIO!! MARIO FOUND MY KEYS!! HOORAY!!" I shouted the good news to the bitter white sky, hopping up and down.

"Here you go," he said proudly. His eyes sparkled with the self-esteem of one who has saved the day.

He was a hero. He ran off, catching up with Pepe and Daniel, and the three of them ran back to the park building to report to John. Victory united them. Fred and I made our way home, my keys resting heavily in my pocket. I was glad that I had lost them so Mario could find them.

"Honey," I said, "We do not know what purposes we serve."

"And in the end, the love you take is equal to the love you make."
- The Beatles

PLANETARY RECOVERY

"I'm from a dysfunctional family." I hear this statement so much these days that I wonder if it has become a new norm. It seems like most people I meet are easily conversant with the idea that some families are organizations that do as much damage as good. And just about everyone is somewhat familiar with the Twelve Steps, because they or someone they know are in recovery for something. There are groups for recovering alcoholics, over eaters, gamblers, incest survivors, abusive parents, codependency, sex and love addiction, compulsive shopping, and people who are too emotional. I'm sure the list is growing and new groups are germinating right now. I wonder if people will start forming support groups for folks who have had serene childhoods so they too can belong. "Hi. My name is Jill. And I come from an ordinary family."

I can understand this. The recovery movement is one of the better opportunities to come along in human society in quite a while. The Twelve Step program offers us what a human being wants most: a chance to begin a spiritual journey with the support of compassionate community, and a chance to come into daily relationship with God on your own terms. It offers structure and support to leave chaos and isolation behind as we conduct a thorough self-inquiry and personal housecleaning. It offers daily practices to establish and deepen serenity, and the joyful duty of serving others who need our help from the full cup of our own experience. So what if you have to make a mess of your life first to join in? Ultimately, the gifts of a long-term active participation in the Twelve Step Program far outweigh the previous anguish of our dysfunction.

In truth, we all come from a large dysfunctional family—the human race. As a whole, we are approaching the point of "hitting bottom" worldwide. Our life here on Planet Earth has become unmanageable. Our ecological problems at this point are so huge, and our society so out of control, that humanity is at the classic decision point—self-destruction or recovery? As in many dysfunctional families, some people are playing the chief role in acting out this destruction, while others live in victimization or denial. People in the recovery and spiritual growth movements are the vanguard of change in the system. Like the family member who begins his or her own recovery long before the addict will admit they have a problem, we can only diligently work our program, speak our truth, witness the inevitable bottom as it comes, and hope for the best outcome.

The recovery and spiritual growth movements may be the evolutionary thrust that leads the human race out of the mess our mass ignorance and addictions have created. Studies in biology reveal that nature improves on her designs through the eons with the experimentation of certain "fringe groups" in a species. A species is going along and maintaining a certain status quo, and somehow a little group becomes isolated from the rest. This group becomes free to experiment and innovate with its food or social habits, and stumbles upon a way that is more efficient and pro-survival. They adopt these ways and teach them to their children. After a few generations, the new way is established, and experiment becomes instinct. Mysteriously, the rest of the species also develops the new way. They "resonate" to the greater strength that has been started in one strand of the community, and evolutionary changes take place worldwide.

The recovery movement certainly began as a "fringe" group. The desperation and social isolation that chronic alcoholics knew in the 1940s set the stage for the new experiment of AA. Those first AA groups built their strength and success in relative isolation from the rest of society. For a long time they were treated with suspicion and misunderstanding by the general public. But they had stumbled upon something that worked, something that was pro-survival. For the first time, alcoholics got better and began to function well in their lives. AA resolutely preserved the purity of the successful elements with strong principles. And the resonance grew. Sunny and simple, AA groups began to spread with the inevitability and persistence of the common dandelion. Now millions of people around the world gather and grow together in AA groups, and the word "recovery" is a common word in today's vocabulary.

I am intrigued with the fast proliferation of addiction-specific clones of the original Twelve Step program. Why is it that there are so many people who are bottoming out on *something?* Why has life become unmanageable for so many people? Maybe the recovery movement is the prelude to something else. It is said that religion is "a finger pointing at the moon," but it is not the moon itself. I have a feeling that recovery too is a finger pointing at something, but it is not the end in itself. There is something else. There is something underneath our species-wide addiction problems that is calling out for evolutionary change.

What is humanity bottoming out on, fundamentally? What are we recovering *towards?* Certainly, we are bottoming out on greed and the gluttonous abuse of resources to the detriment of the planet. I think that we are at the end of a mind-set. Ann Wilson Schaef named it the "white male system," which finds its roots in the patri-archal warrior-cult that overtook societies several thousand years ago. This is a hierarchical, male-dominated model that holds dominance, compe-tition, and control as its chief values. In this model, resources are scarce, and we need to fight somebody to get them so our tribe will be safe. Somebody's always up and somebody's always down, and the world is rife with possible enemies to attack or defend yourself from. Oppression, shame, and exclusion are just part of the game, and the players are always shifting positions— with the exception of women, who have consistently occupied the bottom rung of the ladder throughout the course of this dubious human experiment.

Along with the suppression of the feminine have come some life-threatening side-effects: humans have steadily lost connection with nature, and with the wisdom of the body, feelings, and soul. "Developed" societies are populated with a sea of people who are practically just walking and talking heads, lonely and spiritually malnourished. We turn to some kind of addiction to numb the internal howling that is trying to get our attention and make us face the truth of our situation. If we're very lucky, we bottom out and get into recovery.

In the last half of the twentieth century,

certain fringe groups in our developed societies began experimenting with a new paradigm. Beatniks, hippies, feminists, yoga meditators, "new age" seekers, recovery groups, therapists and people in therapy, holistic healers —one sociologist refers to us as "the cultural creatives." We are the people who have all stepped out of the old mind-set and entered the adventure of creating a new vision for humanity.

The humane and sustainable framework of a new world has been steadily under construction all around us for the last sixty years. It has been created by small circles of people at the fringe, but is now rising front and center in everyone's consciousness. New visions of spiritual health and purposeful living are no longer the sole territory of little support groups in chilly church basements. There is a vast network of groups and individuals around the globe that have added their vibrating cells to a new field of resonance. As the old paradigm and its attendant institutions and systems deconstruct and fade out, it is increasingly important to stand in the new vision.

Where is the new vision living? It lives

everywhere there is a small group that is committed to sturdy joy, world service, love of the Earth, and the alleviation of human suffering.

Time has come full circle for us here on planet Earth. We long for a new world, but it is a world we have known here before. New archeological evidence shows us that societies lived here for thousands of years in peace and wholeness before the bloody times of our recorded history. We used to carry the values of The Mother in our hearts: the values of nurturance, and celebration of a living relationship with a living planet. We need to integrate that ancient sense of wonder and humility into our modern technically-adept consciousness *and take care of everyone.*

We are not fundamentally war-like and messed up by virtue of being human. We're just at the dangerous extreme of our addictions to greed and control over each other and the natural world. We need to get into recovery, collectively. We will grow beyond our chaos and lack of balance. With God's help and a lot of hard work, we will create a future in which the average human being is one who lives in a state of relaxed loving *presence* with the inner self, with others, with planet Earth, and with our Creator. On Earth as it is in Heaven.

The day will come,
when after harnessing the winds,
the tides, and the gravitation,
we will harness for God the energies of love.
And on that day, for the second time
in the history of the world,
man will have discovered fire.
- Teilllhard de Chardin

TRANSFORMATION

I've always believed in the possibility that a major planetary transformation for the better will occur in the course of my lifetime. That belief is sorely tested in these times of worldwide chaos. I watch the media and I see the grim facts and stories parade past my eyes from all points around the world: ignorance, injustice, violence, war, oppression, hunger, disease, pollution, addiction, global warming ... human insanity still appears to reign supreme even though it threatens our collective life. I know that what I see on television is a small percentage of what is actually occurring in the realm of human activity. In fact I am absolutely certain that I am not being shown all the good news and healthy trends that abound at this time in their true proportions. I know this because I can observe directly the active yearning, striving, innovation, and world service going on around me every day, spurred by the basic goodness in the hearts and souls of ordinary people.

Sometimes I wish that a strong wind of truth would blow through the habitual negativity of the media, clear out all the glamour and the garbage, and give us a balanced picture of what's bottom-line *real* about the human situation. I have a friend who refers to the process of truth-telling as "promoting reality." I think it's a slogan worthy of bumper stickers and billboards: "Promote Reality." My friend is a gentle soul, and she has a horror of being invasive or intrusive, but she has made a clear and sturdy commitment to calmly "Promote Reality" in any dysfunctional situation she's in. No matter how thick the ego, aggression, fear, isolation, or denial is in the people around her, this woman tells the truth about the goodness she observes in what is going on, and she promotes solutions that are loving, inclusive, and sustainable. She's not famous and probably never will be, but in her quiet way she has tremendous positive impact in my community because of how she shows up in her work and volunteer activities.

Scientists tell us that the flutter of a butterfly's wing in one part of the globe is an influence on a wind that blows on the other side of the world. Everything is connected and interactive.

With this perspective, I assume that all the fresh energy my friend brings to an arts committee meeting, and all the solid loving *presence* she brings to her work with teenagers at the nearby high school, ripples out from those places and affects me and my endeavors. When a person like my friend shows up to her duties with a healthy mind-set and positive actions, healthy energy is pumped into the system as a whole, increasing the field of possibility that more healthy things can happen. What if more people worldwide made a commitment to truth and loving service, and acted as catalysts of positive transformation when they find themselves in the middle of a dysfunctional situation? The power of such commitment worldwide would have a global effect on what goes on. What if the stories of such personal commitment and the resulting benevolence were amplified by the media instead of all the pain and power plays? What if more of that was considered the "meat" of the news hour? Wouldn't it be great if world leaders and media moguls chose "Promote Reality" as their slogan, as my friend has?

Well, they may never do that. So out of a sense of self-preservation of my hopeful spirit, I choose to leave the TV off most of the time and get my good and bad news directly. The evidence in the human stories all around me inspires belief in an upward trend in humanity, in a way that the media storytellers do not. I draw hope from the people around me that serve with love in humble ways. I draw hope because I myself continue to deepen into new levels of peace and health despite the tragedies and travesties I have endured throughout my life. Restoration of body and soul happens, if you are open to it. Furthermore, I need to look only as far as my city block in South Minneapolis to draw a bold conclusion about the possibility of positive change in the human scene on this planet. In the space of about ten years I watched my block change from a vortex of desperate, ugly chaos to a place of some civility and sustainable living. And believe me, if this block can do it, so can the rest of the planet!

Let me tell you the story. I moved into my charming 1910 house on impulse because we had outgrown our apartment, and a client of mine just about threw it at me for nothing because she was so eager to move out and hadn't been able to sell it. Within a week of living there, we discovered why. The two homes to the south of us were owned by practicing alcoholics who sponsored parties and fights on a regular basis. The four-plex across the street was owned by an absentee landlord who didn't care if his tenants left piles of trash, stolen grocery carts, and neglected toddlers in front of the building. His number was unlisted. The house on the other side of us was occupied by a single mother with seven kids who was too tired and overwhelmed to enforce curfew or civil behavior. Then there was the crack-house down the block with cars pulling up and honking at all hours, and prostitutes slinking against the chain link fence. Oh, and don't forget the steady stream of drunks shouting out after midnight when the corner bar closed, as they staggered their way home down my street.

After a number of sleepless nights that first summer, I bottomed out somewhere in mid-July. I was trapped! I couldn't move out of there because my husband was unemployed and recuperating from a serious injury, and I was in a shaky new business. I felt victimized and ticked off at God, whom I blamed for the situation. One night I cried and raged at God about my miserable fate, and swore hatred and revenge upon my ignorant neighbors. In the middle of my hysteria, God caught my attention for a minute and whispered to me that I was here on purpose, learning some important life lessons. *Lesson No. 1: I must take a stand against the inappropriate behavior of alcoholics.* I come from an alcoholic family, and as a child I learned to adapt to bad behavior passively rather than confront it with power and intelligence. Now it was clear that since I couldn't leave, I would have to take a stand about the quality of my environment. Nothing less than transformation would do!

I approached this challenge on several levels. On a practical level, I put energy into beautifying my property, and picking up garbage whenever it appeared. I calmly and firmly informed my neighbors *every* time their noise kept me awake at night. On a political level, I got acquainted with my neighborhood organizations,

alderman, and Community Crime Prevention. I
wrote letters to landlords; I called the police. On
a spiritual level, I prayed for the lady next door,
the slumlord across the street, and for the block
in general. I forgave everyone for our lifestyle
differences, and prayed that everyone would find
their rightful place. That included me: if God
wanted to lift me up and plant me down in a civilized neighborhood, I was ready to go.

Once a week I went up and down the
block with a bag, picking up garbage. This
was both a practical and a spiritual exercise. I
felt conspicuous and foolish, and angry that I
was taking responsibility for the mess others
had created. I felt nuts doing this for the block
because it seemed as though I was the only one
who cared about it. So I breathed deeply and
thought about Mother Teresa picking up diseased
bodies in Calcutta. She saw God in every one of
those people. I quietly chanted prayers while I
worked, and pretended to see God in everything
too. I practiced a mind-set of loving neutrality as
I picked up sticky junk food wrappers, cigarette
butts, and cans dripping stale beer. I breathed

away judgment of the people who left them there.

After about a month of this, the garbage appeared less and less frequently. The street began to stay clean for weeks at a time. The energy change in the atmosphere was palpable—as if the block itself started breathing easier. Neighbors began emerging from their houses to smile at each other and comment on the change. "Getting better!" we affirmed, any time the chance arose.

Over the next six months, physical changes abounded. The single mother next door became friends with an energetic young man who had a lot of time and talent to help nurture and discipline her kids. The invisible slumlord sold his building to a responsible, accessible man who kicked out the offenders and gave the building a face lift. Both of the landlords who owned houses with alcoholics in them decided to sell, and a sweet gentle woman who loves to garden moved in right next to me, and a lovely family next to her. My gardener neighbor joined with me once a month to pray for the difficult problems and visualize a healthy block. I began to think of my work on the whole block as gardening of sorts—

gardening on many levels.

Before long the crack-house down the street went into foreclosure and was purchased by a man who is really committed to the neighborhood. Over the next two years the city weeded out three of the trashiest houses to cut down on the density. The bar went out of business and a neighborhood committee established a mandate that no bar could ever open there again. In its place is a new restaurant and marketplace. Our small but sturdy block club was given grants to build flower planters, and was also given donations from greenhouses each spring to "green up" the inner city. God had mercy on me and gave me a quiet house on the St. Croix River to escape to on summer weekends, which are still noisy. But it's just city noise, not the crazy dysfunctional noise that frightened me awake each weekend when I first moved in. I can even move out of here now if I really wanted to, but I enjoy the relaxation and family time that my tiny mortgage payment allows me to enjoy.

I am glad that I took a stand for the quality of my experience in my life here, and I believe that the spiritual tools I put to work amplified the effects of what I was doing as an individual, and attracted more people and resources to the cause.

I proved to myself that all it takes is a committed minority to accelerate the rate of positive evolution in any given situation. I kept the point of view that I wasn't alone in my efforts, even if I couldn't always see my cohorts. I chose to believe that the energy I generated as I murmured prayers over garbage and visualized healing light on the crack-house was supported by my friend a few blocks away being patient and firm with an out-of-control teen, and vice versa.

If the forces of restoration can work through a few individuals in a neighborhood like mine and bring it to a new level of health and stability, why can't that be true for our whole planet? The world situation is teetering so evenly between getting better and getting worse, and it's time that more of us add our weight to the constructive momentum, with Spirit's help to amplify each of our small but worthy efforts. Come on, friends—join the movement to "Promote Reality!" The place to change the world is here, in your life, and the time is now. Add a little truth, a little grit, some politics and some prayer. Focus it with your will and deliver it with love. And we shall overcome.

Will transformation.
Oh be inspired for the flame
in which a Thing disappears
and bursts into Something else;
the spirit of re-creation which
masters this earthly form
loves most the pivoting point where
you are no longer yourself.
- Rainer Marie Rilke

Spiritual Commitment

I'm a little weary. I have been living in a gale force wind of growth for a long time. I feel like a beautifully faceted cluster of amethyst that is partially covered with clumps of sand and grit. Some craftsperson in the employment of the Divine is holding me carefully in his hand and blasting away at the grit that hides my beauty with a high-pressure air tool. The grit consists of fear, old sorrows, shame, and rigidity that obscure my radiance and the true shapes and contours of who I am. Some of it flies off easily. Some of it is very stubborn and requires repetitive applications of gentle solvent to gradually work it loose. I am afraid. I am afraid to sparkle unafraid. What about those old voices of shame, what about all those people suffering around the world? But I know that I will let myself keep going full speed ahead into joy and freedom because that's what this whole journey has been about. I am spiritually committed, and Spirit wants me and everyone to shine. *This little light of mine, I'm going to let it shine ....*

That's the trouble when you give yourself wholeheartedly to the practices of self-healing and spiritual evolution and you just stick with them for years and years—eventually they work! I have been on a vigorous spiritual journey for many years. It started with the need to shake loose of the clutches of addiction and unhealthy relationships. I wrestled free of the slavery of shame, and feelings of being undeserving. I left financial struggle and nervous anxiety behind a few miles back. The road is curving into lands of self-esteem, peace, and shining personal success. As I look up the road ahead, I have the eerie sensation that the picture is turning from black and white into full color. Where's the fear? I'm afraid because I see no fear there! I want to sit down on the road where it still looks familiar and cuddle up to an old problem or two. Gee, Toto—I don't think we're in Kansas anymore!

When I was a child I stopped my playing in awe one day to see a black man on television speaking to a lot of people. His radiant face and awesome oration spoke of his dream for a world without hate or suffering. My hair stood up all over my body and rivers of tingles bathed me as tears streamed steadily down my face. I realized that this man was working in service of the Truth. I wanted to do that too. I understood then that the only thing that really mattered to me was to grow up to be wise and free, and to help other people do so too. I am a spiritual worker. Now my prayer is to accept the real possibility that I will reap the fruits of this commitment. The time for fulfillment is here.

I have given myself to the cause of the evolution of human consciousness. I work on my own consciousness by being obedient to the healing directions coming from my Higher Self, and as I master a facet of it, people begin to come to me for help with the very same issue. There are people ahead of me on the continuum of consciousness. They guide and inspire me to greater self-mastery, as I hope to guide and inspire others. It's not a hierarchy of being better than someone else. It's more like the color spectrum of white light seen through a prism—a continuum of consciousness vibrating in different colors, yet all parts of one Being.

I want you to give yourself wholeheartedly to the evolution of human consciousness too. Starting in your own life today, make an athletic leap to the higher ground that you know is calling you. There is no more room, no more time for fear or withholding from Truth and Love in our world. Come forward! Break out of the bondage of fear and control, and surrender to the flow of sharing your love and inner beauty in your daily engagements. All the help you could possibly need to do all this is right here, right now. Agree to shine in service of Truth. Become committed.

A better world will not arise out of the manipulation of existing political and economic forms. It will happen out of a shift in our consciousness as a whole. The relationship of form to consciousness is like the relationship of plants and soil. If you significantly alter the pH balance in the soil, old plants will die out and different ones will thrive. We are changing the pH balance of humanity's consciousness by composting our fears, and planting seeds of love and selfless service. A new world is coming in a mysterious manner we can barely predict, and cannot control. It may take many more years for this shift to be complete, but it's coming. All we can do is submit joyfully to our uncomfortable role as evolutionary mutations in our species.

I know of a fine spiritual teacher whose journey took him from a small village in India to a meditation path in the Himalayas. He was then led to do political work for the Indian government. He worked long and hard with the best minds and resources available to address the problems of hunger and poverty there. He concluded at last that these efforts would be ultimately ineffective until there was a large-scale change in human consciousness for them to take root in and flourish. He now teaches meditation and The Course in Miracles to twenty serious students, who then teach it to others. Occasionally he goes into periods of retreat for extended meditation. He is a spiritual worker.

In the 1970s, three spiritual masters from different meditation traditions left their homelands to teach meditation on a large scale to seekers around the world. One of them, Baba Muktananda of India, said that the voice of his guru commanded him to do this and be part of a revolution of consciousness. When asked why this was happening now, he replied simply, "Sometimes such a time comes." He is a spiritual worker.

Mother Teresa was another person who had a powerful impact in our era. She served the poorest of the poor in the streets of Calcutta, encouraging us to perform "small acts with great love." Why do we respect that so much? Because our spiritual instincts tell us that she chose to walk on higher ground, even though the way was difficult. Someone is inviting us to walk there too.

The higher ground is different for everyone. Most of us are not as awe-inspiring as Mother Teresa, and the television cameras will probably never find us and celebrate our work. But if we choose our spiritual duties and perform them with love, our work will attract grace, and it will promote the evolution of consciousness. Maybe your duty is to be the best parent you can be. Maybe you will volunteer in a Walk for Aids or be a Big Brother or Big Sister. You could make a commitment to pray more often, or to improve your diet, or to get into therapy, or to be more honest with your loved ones. It all goes into the same pool of human consciousness. Every bit of your self-effort and world service helps everyone else with theirs.

Our world today is like a lovely old house that is in serious disrepair because it has been destroyed by drunken tenants living in ignorance and disrespect of themselves and others. There is garbage everywhere, broken windows, and holes punched in walls. On the continuum of consciousness, people who are healing themselves are like individuals that have stopped participating in the destruction, and are getting their bearings. Spiritual workers are like a sturdy work crew descending on the house on a long Saturday with their sleeves rolled up. We intend to clean it up and repair the damage and restore the house to its original glory, with some thoughtful modern improvements. And everywhere around us people are stepping forward with the resources, the technologies, and the commitment to end unnecessary human suffering and to discover how to live in right relationship with Earth and with Spirit.

Is it worth it? Can you really make a difference? Yes! Let's have you in here with both feet, bringing your friends along for reinforcement, and we'll all keep going until we get it right. Will you be committed too?

"This is total surrender:
to be what God asks you to be.
To accept that you are in the street
if God wants you to be in the street—
to accept that you are in the palace,
if God wants you to be in the palace.
To give whatever He asks you to give
whether you are in the street or in the palace—
and to give it with a big smile.
This is the surrender to God."
- Mother Teresa

Waiting For a Raft to Appear

The three of them were sprawled sideways across the yellow raft, heads flung back, mouths wide open with howls of laughter. Squashed together like sardines, Savannah, James, and Zoe tipped and teetered giddily while they sought balance between them in a rubber raft made for two people. James' long legs disappeared into the water on one side of the boat, and his lengthy torso extended well over the rim of the other side. But the two short girls at either elbow were slouched down inside it, their bottoms grazing the stony shore through the thin rubber. Zoe's long black braids trailed in the water, floating like seaweed as the raft bobbed dangerously low to the shining surface. It was already starting to ship plenty of river water. Savannah's face was red and wet with tears of laughter, but she tried to pull it together for a moment as I stood nervously on the shore and attempted to talk some sense into them.

"Um ... guys? This really might be kind of a bad idea ... you might want to think about this, it's a long trip to be so crowded ... Savannah? Where are the oars?"

"We ... *ha ha ha* ... don't have any ... *ha ha ha* ... don't worry—Mary, I think it's going to be just *fine!*"

"You don't have *oars*? I thought you were kidding about that!"

The boat began to drift languidly out from the shore, coaxed by the strong current that runs in the middle of the river. James and Zoe attempted to synchronize their wobbles as they bailed out the water in the bottom. They were about twenty feet away from me. I could still put my foot down and say *Absolutely not! I won't let you do this.* But they were seventeen, they knew everything, and they wanted an adventure. I was vulnerable to losing this argument because I wanted them to like me and think I'm cool. I was seventeen once.

"Mary, it's okay," Savannah said, making more of an effort to assure me. "The river's not deep. The current will take us home. We really want to do this. We'll be fine."

"But Sav! I told your Mom I was driving you two miles up-river. I think we came a lot further than that because we couldn't find the landing we thought was there. I have no idea how far up we came or how long this will take you. This will be much longer than two hours. You'd better reconsider this since you don't have oars."

"*Ha ha ha!* Cut it out, James! Oops! Um ... Mary ... we don't have anything we have to do all day; it doesn't matter if it takes a lot of hours. It's what we want to do."

"But you have no shirts!" I whined. "No hats! No sunscreen! No *oars,* for God's sake! I didn't *know* that!"

"We've got these," Zoe said. She sat up and earnestly feigned preparedness. She waved a plastic bag over her head. It had three peanut butter sandwiches in it. "And this!" she cried triumphantly, holding up a half-empty bottle of water.

"Great," I muttered sullenly. The raft drifted further out and downstream, slowly, inevitably.

"Savannah!" I shouted. "This is your last chance to change your mind! You might hate this after a while and you'll be stuck! Listen to your intuition right now this minute and tell me if you really feel you ought to do this!"

"*Ha, ha, ha ... uh ... OK ...*" (Silence.) "MARY—IT WILL BE *FINE!*" They drifted away.

Defeated, I walked dejectedly back to my car. My mind was going crazy, but truly, the inside part of me felt comfortable. I, too, thought that it was probably fine. Foolish, maybe, but not dangerous. Nevertheless, I practiced my conversation with Sav's mother Lois, my best friend, on my return ride home. *It was a little further than we said ... I know it isn't the best, but I don't think they're in any real danger ... my intuition and theirs were OK with it ... Lois, they really wanted to do it ....* My reasoning seemed to grow more lame by the mile as I watched the odometer tick off the actual distance we had driven, through thickly wooded country, to where I let them off at a landing. Oh, Lord. It was *nine* miles, not two.

Lois' usual calm demeanor deepened to a

graver set, and her voice was gently incredulous as she looked up at me from the county map we anxiously hovered over.

"Nine miles, and no oars? No shoes, no shirts, no sunscreen? Mary, there's nothing between here and there but miles of brushy county forest! What if they get tired of the river, and try to get out and walk home? They might get lost. And I don't even know their parents that well."

I looked at her miserably. I hadn't thought of that. I knew Lois understood that I made important decisions by intuition, and we both appreciated a kid's need for adventure. We raised our rowdy daughters together since they were tots with a shared understanding about that sort of thing when it came to safety guidelines. But what *would* I say to Zoe and James' parents, or the sheriff for that matter, about dumping three bare-foot kids in bathing suits into the river nine miles upstream in a little raft with no supplies?

I vowed reparation. I called the park district to find out how fast the current in the St. Croix River runs; Lois and I calculated that the river would bring them to our landing in about six hours, if all went well. Since it could be dark by then, I also called the sheriff to ask him at what point it made sense to declare someone lost on the river. I went home and worried devotedly while I baked muffins for them and packed a generous picnic supper. I had already assured Lois that I would wait for them with her at the landing all evening, if that's what it took. She graciously accepted all my efforts at reparation.

A few hours before sunset, Lois and I headed for our rendezvous point, well supplied with food, books, flashlights, and conversation subjects. The light was clear and golden on the blue river as we made our way to a large boulder that sat in the shallows about ten feet from shore. The rock accommodated the two of us snugly, and we settled in for our vigil. Across the river, a fishing bird plunged into the water with a *splash* and flew off with something silver flashing in its beak. The river flowed around us, unperturbed by this event or any, at three miles an hour.

Lois and I talked a lot, then less and less. We worked through all the best and worst scenarios. They wouldn't drown because the river wasn't deep and they all knew how to swim. There were no rapids in the river's course between those two landings. They probably wouldn't be murdered by a psychopathic hunter or fisherman—that kind of thing was only in bad movies. The biggest concern was that they would get bored or confused, and get off the river to come home on foot. That wouldn't be good because they were barefoot and wearing only wet bathing suits, and the nights were cool enough now in early September to cause concern about hypothermia. Lois and I would have to face the embarrassment of calling the sheriff and requesting a search party, and be in big trouble with the other parents. (Presumably the other parents were more sensible than me and sure to be angry that I let them go on the river like that.) Of course, they'd be found. This was Wisconsin for God's sake, not the Himalayas. We worried anyway.

The color of sky and river deepened. We strained our sight steadily ahead, seeking a glimpse of our watery wayfarers, but the river bent out of sight less than a mile away, so our further vision was thwarted. We heard news of them from a fisherman going by in a motorboat. "Oh, yes! I saw 'em!" he said. "They were having a great time ... laughing every minute .... No, that was quite a ways back. It'll be a while."

He motored off downstream, leaving us alone with each other and the river, peacefully flowing at exactly the same rate. Silence grew as the sun disappeared from the sky. Slowly, delicately, the chilly white mists emerged from both banks of the river, like forest spirits venturing forth for the night, seeking a rendezvous with each other over the water. It was a little scary, and very lovely. Lois and I looked at our watches, and made an agreement about when the real panic could begin. The river didn't know what time it was. We cuddled beneath a rough wool blanket together, waiting.

We heard them long before we saw them. Howls of laughter drifted to us from the distance, their unmistakable hilarity ricocheting around the soft corners of the river bend. How could they be laughing and conversing with each other so *loudly?* We could practically make out their

words even though we couldn't see them yet, and
we knew for a fact that they were wedged right up
close to each other's eardrums. How could they
still be laughing after six hours on a crowded,
ill-prepared river journey? It cracked us up. Lois
and I laughed too, silently, so they wouldn't
hear us, as we lay in wait for them. We laughed
harder and harder until tears streamed down our
faces, clinging to each other for balance so we
wouldn't fall off our perch into the river. The river
murmured against our rock, unknowing.

It took forever for the tiny black dot
against the grey river-and-sky backdrop to grow
large enough to look like a raft bursting with
three teenagers in bathing suits. They kept getting
caught on the edge near the grassy banks, too far
from the current to make the kind of haste we
felt was appropriate at this point. If they only
had *oars* ...! Oh well. Lois and I kept our silence,
blending conspiratorially into the rock in the dim
light. We wanted to hear every silly word out of
their mouths before they realized someone was
listening. Eventually they had a long, hushed
discussion with each other about whether there

really were figures on that rock or not, until with a hoot and a hey they recognized the landing. When they finally discerned that it was us sitting there on the rock laughing at them, they were mortified.

Savannah, James, and Zoe floundered stiffly out of their cramped positions and into the cold, dark shallows. They reached the haven of the shore one by one, dragging their yellow raft limply behind them. We adults hugged them and applied emergency muffins while we took an uncompromising inventory of their condition. They were cold, shoulders hunched up to their ears, and teeth chattering. They were sunburned. They were hungry. They were triumphant, but very glad to be rescued. They were ... *fine.* That river current flowed in the very heart of me for days and days afterwards.

And I say to you that all shall be well,
and all shall be well, and all shall be well,
and thou shalt see that all manner of things shall be well.
- Julian of Norwich

OTHER WORKS BY MARY HAYES GRIECO

*The Kitchen Mystic: Spiritual Lessons Hidden in
    Everyday Life*
Hazelden Educational Materials 1992

Audio Books on Cassette Tape (2-tape sets)
*The Kitchen Mystic: Spiritual Lessons Hidden in
    Everyday Life*
*The Peaceful Heart: A Practical Guide to Unconditional
    Love and Forgiveness*
*A Woman's Ways:
    Women's Spirituality and
    Develop Your Intuition*
Living Your Purpose

Audio Books on CD
*The Peaceful Heart: A Practical Guide to Unconditional
    Love and Forgiveness*
*A Woman's Ways:
    Women's Spirituality and
    Develop Your Intuition*

Purchase these works at
www.maryhayesgrieco.com

Mary Hayes Grieco is a respected spiritual teacher based in Minneapolis, Minnesota. She has served as a light and an inspiration to thousands of people since she first began teaching spirituality classes in 1982. Mary was the creator and host of her own local radio show, *The Blue Couch,* from 1986–1994, and was a columnist for *The Phoenix Health and Recovery Journal.* Her first book, *The Kitchen Mystic: Spiritual Lessons Hidden in Everyday Life,* was published by Hazelden in 1992. This book and subsequent works (*The Peaceful Heart, Living Your Purpose, and A Woman's Ways*) were published as audio books by HiBridge Audio in 1996. Mary served on the faculty of Hazelden Renewal Center as a spiritual retreat leader from 1993-2008. From 1996-2003 she taught courses in the spirituality of the workplace at The Management Center at the University of St. Thomas in Minneapolis.

Mary met her mentor, Dr. Edith Stauffer, PhD, in 1986, and entered intensive training as a student and teacher of UNCONDITIONAL LOVE AND FORGIVENESS, Edith's life work which has become Mary's as well. She has taught this powerful method of emotional healing since 1990 in a wide variety of venues— churches, hospitals, businesses, treatment centers, and professional conferences—locally, nationally, and internationally. Mary has taught Forgiveness in both the Republic of Ireland and in the North of Ireland, and she was a featured speaker at the Nobel Peace Prize Forum in 2005. Mary is currently the director and lead trainer of The Midwest Institute for Forgiveness Training, which provides programs for professionals, the general public, and committed students of self-mastery.

Mary thinks of herself as a philosopher and healer, and a lover of God in ordinary things. She is dedicated to liberating the joy of the human spirit and participating fully in what she perceives to be the birth of a new humanity. Mary encourages us to do our part by healing our wounds with Forgiveness, and illuminating our consciousness with steady spiritual habits. She hopes that you too will "be a light" and live purposefully in service to others in these transformational times.